Stories, stories everywhere

*With gratitude and affection to my family
and friends who have been such faithful
travelling companions and to the storytellers
and story-listeners who have generously
shared their gifts along the way.*

Stories, stories everywhere

∞ Good practice for storytellers ∞

Sandra Pollerman

∞

Text copyright © Sandra Pollerman 2001
The author asserts the moral right
to be identified as the author of this work

Published by
The Bible Reading Fellowship
First Floor, Elsfield Hall,
15–17 Elsfield Way, Oxford OX2 8FG
ISBN 1 84101 142 8

First published 2001
10 9 8 7 6 5 4 3 2 1 0
All rights reserved

Acknowledgments
Unless otherwise stated, scripture quotations are taken from The New Revised
Standard Version of the Bible, Anglicized Edition, copyright © 1989, 1995 by
the Division of Christian Education of the National Council of the Churches
of Christ in the USA, and are used by permission. All rights reserved.

A catalogue record for this book is available from the British Library

Printed and bound in Great Britain by
Omnia Books Limited, Glasgow

Foreword

In the midst of the relationship between story, storyteller and listener, there lies sacred space. Here we create a meeting place where human and divine can mingle together. Inhabiting this space can be a transforming experience for all who are present.

Stories are gifts and this book is, indeed, a treasury of gifts shared by Sandra Pollerman with each and every one of us. Here is a wealth of wisdom and inspiration, practical ideas and detailed examples. We are empowered to tell our stories and are given the tools to enable us to share these gifts and to say, 'I can do it!'

Whether teacher or preacher, parent or priest, in home, school or parish there is an invitation on offer to share our story. So, bottle of bubbles at the ready, some pebbles in our pocket, voice warmed up, here we go...

Alison Seaman
Director, The National Society's Religious Education Centre

Contents

Introduction

I didn't start out to be a storyteller; it just sort of happened to me. In fact, I was keenly moving in another direction when there was a terrible accident and I was left quite wounded, lost, confused. It might have been worse but necessity kept me functioning and then a friend came to encourage me on. 'I need some help,' was the way she began. Beverley Mathias was children's officer for the National Book League at the time. 'I need someone to tell stories at an event which I'm organizing and I think you'd be good at it. Will you come?'

As I considered the request, I realized I *did* know some stories. My grandmother had told me all our family stories. My father worked as a travelling salesman and had blessed me with 'the gift of the gab'. I had used stories very effectively in my classroom teaching days, and my own children always had a story at bedtime. So, in order to help my friend out, I collected some of my favourite stories, put some props and stuffed toys in a carrying bag, and went to tell stories at the event.

I had a good time. The listening group grew as I 'told'. Everyone had a bit of a laugh and nobody was too frightened at the scary bits. When my spot was finished, I received a most affirming response. My friend's boss came up to me, smiling broadly. 'You were a lot better than we thought you would be,' he said. 'Here's some money. Would you be willing to do it again?'

I did do it again… and again, and again, and it still goes on. This unexpected invitation offered me a beginning which has enabled me to travel over three continents and six of the seven seas. As I have watched and listened, I have claimed new stories. As I have shaped and shared this material with people from different backgrounds with various senses of humour, all our lives have been touched. Storytelling is a shared, corporate experience. It is composed of the listener, the teller and the tale itself. As we participate, we occupy each of the roles in the process.

The ongoing experience of becoming a storyteller has led me into places of healing, along pathways leading to the building up of community, and into relationship with a loving creator God. The experience continues to deepen my faith and encourage hope for the future. Sharing stories with other people has also released a tear or two, and not a little laughter.

To claim the story to tell, and then to shape it and share it, is the work of the storyteller. There are nearly as many 'right ways' to complete this process as there are people who undertake it. None the less, it can be helpful to experiment with some basic techniques in the development of an individual style. It is also true that different patterns of preparation are useful when working with different types of story material—for example, fairy tales, tall tales, narrative, parables, psalms and so on.

The following chapters begin at the beginning and follow through the process. Chapter 1 deals with the choosing of a story. Chapters 2, 3 and 5 continue through various appropriate patterns for shaping material. Chapters 4, 7 and 8 offer tips and techniques for sharing stories in a variety of situations and the effective use of props and material. Chapter 9 presents one approach to using storytelling as the focus of a programme of religious education. Chapter 10 offers a final reflection and a parting gift.

When I asked a friend about how he thought I should end the book, he responded, 'I heard a funny story about endings!' and so it goes on.

Through this book I would like to extend to you the invitation I once heard: 'I need some help.' The listening audience around us is growing. Many are waiting to hear the stories of who we are and how we came to be here. The encouragement and hope that lie within our sacred tradition need hands and voices to help with the telling. There are tales of danger and challenge met which must not be forgotten. 'I need someone to help me tell these stories. I think you'd be good at it.'

Teachers, preachers, adults and children… you probably are already good at it. Even so, the chapters in this book each deal with some of the improvements I've learned to make along the way. Telling stories and passing them on is very much a part of our faith tradition and spiritual heritage.

Some stories say that as the people of God travelled through the wilderness, they told stories. Periodically they would stop to rest and refresh themselves; they would replenish their supplies, celebrate new life among them, bury their dead. At such significant points it was the custom to build a small cairn of stones to mark their passage. Others who passed by would sometimes add another stone, with respect and solidarity for other travellers.

Please consider each of the chapters in this book as such a cairn. As you pause to read through the work, I hope you find refreshment, discovering new ways to tell the story and celebrate life. For all that seems worn out and lifeless, feel free to leave it behind. Many of the ideas and materials discussed in the book have grown out of gifts shared and developed with other tellers and artists and friends. So, please also feel free to carry with you as you continue on your own journey the ideas which seem to resonate and grow with you. Leave a thought behind, to continue the collection of gratitude and respect for all those who pass this way.

CHAPTER ONE

ϾϿ

God's story, our story

Whenever we come together to share our faith,
we end up telling stories.

M.E. MOYNAHAN SJ, *ONCE UPON A PARABLE*, P. 8.

In this chapter, we will explore this process. The sections include:
❖ thoughts on getting started
❖ finding 'story starts' in simple objects
❖ choosing a story

Getting started

Telling a story is different from reading it off the page. We don't have the words in front of us or the safety barrier of even a sheet of paper between us and the listeners. We make eye contact with the listeners and it is definitely a shared experience. Yet it isn't really the same as a conversation where the thoughts of the moment are spoken.

Telling a story is also different from repeating a memorized script. We are invited to identify ourselves in the story being contemplated, to reappropriate who we are now, and who we shall or can be, in terms of the story. Its movements, transactions, transformation, become ours. It is important to be faithful to the story we have received, particularly so with biblical material. And yet our interaction with the story is not a static relation of confrontation with images of virtue or vice; we are not addressed by finished pictures, of a quality once and for all achieved and so no longer 'taking time'. Rather, our relationship to the text is an active working through of the story's movement in our own time.[1]

As communicators of a faith tradition, we tell stories we have received from those who have gone before us. As we pass them on in turn, they carry the implications of our own lived experiences. These stories of God and God's people bear the traces of time— the times of the people within which the stories began, through generations of retelling, up to the present moments of our corporate sharing. As we 'take time' to prepare and present this material, God's story and our story come together.

Biblical narrative can be imaginatively retold from a first- or third-person point of view. Sensitive work with parables can draw teller and listener alike deeper into the mystery of the creator. Many of the stories in the Bible are very detailed but others offer only brief sketches. When we suggest explanations of what might have been left out, the stories which unfold are called *midrash* in Hebrew.[2]

Something is definitely lost if the telling doesn't flow through the filter of personal experience. The story of David and Goliath, or the baptism of Jesus, or even the feeding of the five thousand, become more relevant and compelling when told out of the awareness that, at some level, the teller's own lived experience is informed and enabled by these moments from our faith tradition.

Story 'starts' with simple things

It is not always easy to find the first story to tell. Especially when beginning to work with personal experience, there is sometimes an uncertainty about sharing in an appropriate and balanced manner. The exercises which follow explore ways to begin to become less self-conscious about claiming the particulars of everyday experience as story 'starts'. These exercises work for individuals; they are also useful for enabling group process.

Something you have with you

You can try the first one right now, even if you're reading this on the train or in a waiting-room. Select something you have with you right now—something that you have with you for a reason. It might be something you are carrying in a pocket or bag. If you're at home, it might be something near you on the desk or the table beside the place where you're sitting. It might be something you're wearing... perhaps a piece of jewellery or even your shoelace. Choose something you have with you *for some reason*.

Take the object in your hands. Finger it, roll it around in your palms. Let yourself get the feel of it. I suggest that your connection with this object forms the seed of a story. In order to release this story, consider the following questions:

❖ Where did this object come from?

❖ Why do you have it with you?

❖ If you could predict, what do you think might happen to this object in the future, or what do you hope might become of it?

Take a few minutes to let the memory of your experience replay itself in your thinking.

Now, how would you retell the story of this object? Perhaps you can tell yourself the story, maybe out loud. Perhaps it would help to imagine you have a person sitting next to you and begin by actually showing them the object. Give yourself two or three minutes to retell the story. Be guided by the questions listed above. Begin with where the object came from. Let the reason you carry it with you form the body of the story. Let your prediction or hope for the future bring the story to a close.

I like to use this exercise with a group. It is at this point that I invite the members to choose partners and to move into spaces where they can quietly speak to each other. The objects people carry with them really do have meaning for individuals, and as we begin to share these stories with others, we claim more of our own experience and learn more about those with whom we work and play.

Very often, when I need to have a partner to balance the numbers in the exercise, I will choose to share the story of one of the rings I like to wear. It was given to me by a friend when I was not very well. It is a wide band, made of silver, and has ten small raised flowers moulded on it. My friend said that each flower represented one of her prayers for me and that when I wanted to, I could say my prayers that way too. Wearing the ring gave me comfort, and as I convalesced I did use my ring as a thinking ring, if not always for prayer.

During one workshop as I was sharing that story, the person I was working with began to grin very broadly. 'My grandmother used to wear a ring not unlike that one, and I haven't seen one like it in a long time. She called it a "decade ring" and said it had been used to help people remember to say their prayers.' It is a wonder to me to discover the way we connect with other people and the world around us. As we share our stories, such connections become evident and our communities become stronger.

Something you find outdoors

One way to extend or reapply this exercise is to take a short walk outside. Spend the time in the garden, or wander through a wooded or open commons area. Maybe you live near a lake or the sea; perhaps the area outside where you are is fully paved and lined with shops! The idea is to interact with your natural environment. Look at what is growing or lying around or blowing about. Choose an object that you see—a stone or a piece of wood; a feather or a shell; even a piece of glass or a stray piece of rubbish.

Bring your object inside and take time to look at it more closely. Consider how your object has been formed. How does it look and feel? With what qualities is your object endowed? Is it firm or flexible, hard or soft? Is it delicate or durable, heavy or lightweight?

Notice the designs or patterns that may be there. Take note of the colours, any visible markings, signs of use and wear or weathering. Hold the object up to the light and turn it round and round. How do the light and shadow play across your object? Does it look different in different light? Is there a definite inside or outside, top or bottom, front or back? What do you notice about your object that you have not seen or thought about before?

Now 'switch on' your imagination. Let yourself wonder about what tale this object might be able to tell or perhaps what story or personal experience it suggests to you. Follow the process as before, being guided by three similar questions.

❖ Where might the object have come from?
❖ What circumstances might have brought it to that spot?
❖ If you could predict, or the object could somehow let it be known, what might happen to the object in the future?

For a storyteller, this is a useful kind of exercise for stimulating creative connections. Sometimes a simple process of wondering about an object can provide an interesting introduction to a longer tale. Musing about a treasure found in the ground could lead to a retelling of the Bible story of the person who found a treasure in a field (Matthew 13:44). A stone, shell, or piece of water-weathered wood could lead to the story of how God saved the children of Israel from the Egyptians (Exodus 14:19–30). A feather might suggest trusting in God and lead to a poem or quiet prayer.

Hildegard of Bingen, a very creative woman of the Middle Ages, included such an image in her writings. She saw that a feather flew, not because of anything in itself but because the air bore it along. 'Thus am I...' she said, 'a feather on the breath of God.'[3]

Identifying one from another

Another application of such an exercise leads to the discovery of the uniqueness of a single item among a collection of objects of a similar nature. Do you have a bag of marbles? A pocketful of change? A mug full of pencils and pens? Even a handful of tea-spoons from the cutlery drawer will work. Spread this array of things which are similar-but-not-quite-the-same in front of you. Choose one that catches your attention.

Take the object you've chosen and hold it in your hand. Turn it round and round. How does it look? How does it feel? What comes to mind when you hold an object like this? Now look at it a bit more closely. Notice the marks and patterns on the surface. What colours do you see? Now hold your object up to the light. Does it look different with the light behind it, reflecting off the surface, shining through it? How do the patterns of light and shadow play on the surface?

Does anything about this object remind you of yourself? Has something happened to you, or have you accomplished something, which comes to mind when you look at or hold this object? What are the most qualifying marks on the object? If you had to replace it in the bag, pocket, mug or drawer and later select it as your own, how could you tell it was yours? What marks would immediately remind you of its unique qualities?

Could you share something of the story of this object... in only three minutes?! As you reflect on what you might say, be guided by the following three questions:

❖ Why did you select this particular marble/coin/spoon?
❖ What story does this object bring to mind, or how is it particularly like you (or different from you)?
❖ If you had to return this object to its fellows and later reclaim it, how would you know it was yours?

When I use this exercise with a group, this is the point at which individuals are invited to choose partners with whom to share the story of their object. In giving the directions for the next part of the exercise, it is possible to refocus the role of the storyteller as well as to clarify the role of the listener. If you want to try using this exercise with a group, this is a pattern you might follow.

Clarify the listening role

A story sharing requires the integration of the teller and the listener and the tale itself. Often the significant role of the listener is overlooked. To continue, invite each pair to decide between themselves who will be the first *teller* and who the first *listener*.

During the few minutes that you offer the tellers for recalling their three-minute 'story bite' about the object they have chosen, turn the attention of the others to the role of the listener. Invite the listeners to be willing to turn their whole attention to the story being told—to 'listen with intent'. As the story unfolds, it often resonates with the listener's own experience. Such harmonies seem to be a gift of the story itself and draw the teller and the listener closer together. It is appropriate for the listener to notice and store this for later feedback. As the listener becomes more connected with the tale, the teller receives additional energy and affirmation to continue with the sharing. Mutual involvement in an unfolding story deepens and enhances the experience in unspoken but none the less recognizable ways.

These questions can be useful to the listener to both focus and reflect on their own listening skills:

❖ Were you able to catch the story your partner was sharing as a whole?

❖ Did it resonate with your own experience?

❖ What is one quality of your partner's ability as a storyteller which made it easy for you to listen?

Reflect on the telling

The reflection process is as significant for the teller as it is for the listener. The teller's job is to present the story in such a way that the listener's own experience and imagination are engaged. It is important for the teller to be aware of the possible indicators of the listener's involvement. Physical postures, facial characteristics and audible responses can all provide useful clues. Laughter and even very deep silences help the teller to gauge the degree of interaction between the listener and the story itself.

As tellers, we also need to become 'self-listeners'. Developing an ongoing awareness of the rhythm, pitch and modulation of our own vocal characteristics is important. Attentiveness to diction and enunciation can help us individually to improve interaction with both the story and the listener. Unconscious, artificial vocal patterns can separate the teller and the listeners and impede the flow of even well-prepared material. It is, therefore, also important to take some time to evaluate our own presentation after each bit of storytelling we undertake.

The following questions can offer a very simple guide to begin that process:

- ❖ Did the telling go as you expected?
- ❖ How did the listeners respond to the presentation?
- ❖ At what point were the listeners really involved with the development of the story?
- ❖ Were you able to adapt the length of the story to meet the needs of the moment?
- ❖ What did *you* enjoy most about the experience?
- ❖ Were you able to go through the story without being lost or distracted?
- ❖ Did the words you spoke seem to flow smoothly?
- ❖ What adjustments did you make in your personal presentation as you moved through the story?
- ❖ If you were to tell this story again, what details would you leave out? What additions might you include?

Choosing a story

If you've worked through the previous exercises, you have perhaps already begun to discover how very many stories there are waiting to be told. Even more importantly, you've probably noticed that you recognize many of them, have lived through quite a few, and have been told even more. Truly, there are stories everywhere. So the problem becomes not whether there are stories worth telling but which one to choose!

Perhaps the previous exercises have also planted the seed of understanding that the needs and experience of the listener as well as the dynamic of the story itself are contributing factors in making a harmonious choice.

Sometimes the story chooses you

A folk tale from the native tradition of Australia suggests, 'Story hide behind rock. Wait 'til good teller come along. Then story jump in teller's brain so quick... so quietly... teller think story his own idea!'

Sometimes it seems to happen just like that. A story you read, or hear, or remember from family tradition seems to stay in your memory. Perhaps you become aware that you have one in mind that you've been carrying around for a long time. Accept the gift. Choose stories to tell that appeal to you, resonate with your own experience, seem easy to remember.

Sometimes the story is chosen for you

In the book of Ezekiel, the prophet reports: 'The Lord God said to me, O mortal, eat what is offered to you; eat this scroll, and go, speak to the house of Israel' (Ezekiel 3:1).

We may not receive such a direct revelation of material, yet as teachers and preachers in the Church we might be asked to work with the year's lectionary and pattern of readings. When working in the education system or even offering a contribution to a larger event, very often the theme is prescribed and there is a particular story which seems most appropriate. Claim it as your own. You may have choice over the translation from which you work and surely over the words you use in the retelling. The Ezekiel passage continues: 'So I opened my mouth, and he gave me the scroll to eat... and in my mouth it was as sweet as honey' (3:2–3).

It can be a very releasing moment on a storyteller's journey to agree to retell, rather than re-read, a set story from the Bible or a preferred story from a book. The exercises in the next chapters will explore ways to take a text from scripture, a story out of a book, and retell it authentically—without 'tearing the pages', so to speak. The commitment of the teller is to retell authentically the story that has been received.

Sometimes the choice really is your own

'Spoiled for choice' is the phrase that springs to mind. As you continue to tell and retell and accumulate a personal repertoire of preferred tales, you will also collect a frame of reference for making the critical choice. These suggestions may be a beginning.

Consider the purpose of the event

Stories are said to entertain, teach, and lead in to an experience of worship. A narrative can give voice to unspoken hopes and longings and offer a possible pattern out of chaos. The action and inter-action of archetypal figures can offer healing and release; laughter and tears accompany the process. A particular fairy tale or a story from traditional folklore may have wide application if the retelling is tailored to the purpose of the event. The pattern of presentation may focus on the entertaining, educational or worshipful aspect of a story, but the story well told will very likely invite its own response in the heart and mind of the listener.

Identify a profile of the listening group

The age, size and orientation of the listening group are significant factors in the selection and presentation of material. In my experience, I have found it true that a story well told has a cradle-to-grave appeal; none the less, each gathering has special needs. It is important to choose language, imagery and materials that are appropriate. For example, the story of the good shepherd has relevance for the whole faith community; sensitive choice of language and detail in the telling will allow even young children as well as adults to enter the story out of their own experience.

Choose a story you enjoy

We sometimes find it hard to give ourselves permission to really choose and explore the things we enjoy; in this instance, the 'pleasure principle' is an asset. It may be easier to remember a story you like. It may also be easier to work with a favoured piece of material, over time, to shape it and refine the presentation for sharing. Even after such preparation, your own delight in the material is likely to be communicated to the listener through your telling and draw the listener more easily into the listening space.

Take seriously the allotted time for the telling

The length of the story and the time set aside for its telling need to fit together. It is possible to reshape even a long story to be told in a small timeframe, but the richness of the tale may be lost in the process. Expanding a slight tale to fill a longer timeframe may also prove unsatisfactory. Experience, and sometimes necessity, suggest the adaptation of material during the telling. An experienced teller may capitalize on moments where the listening group is really enjoying a detail, or hasten through an unexpected 'misfit' when the expected response is not forthcoming. However, one of the most significant lessons experience teaches is the significance of closing well and finishing in good time.

NOTES

1 Rowan Williams, now Anglican Bishop of Monmouth, introduces and discusses this understanding in Williams, R., 'The Literal Sense of Scripture', *Modern Theology 7:2*, January 1991, pp. 121–125.

2 A basic explanation of *midrash* can be found in Bradt SJ, Kevin M., *Story as a Way of Knowing*, Sheed & Ward, USA, 1997, p. 174: '*Midrash* can be thought of in two ways. First, it names and defines a process of interpreting the Bible and, on occasion, other sacred texts. *Midrash* also refers to the whole corpus of work which has collected these interpretations. The term *midrash* can identify both an activity and a literature.'

 Also, in Sasso, Sandy Eisenberg, *But God Remembered: Stories of Women from Creation to the Promised Land*, Jewish Lights Publishing, 1995, about *midrash* Rabbi Sasso says, 'When we read the Bible we often wonder about what has been left out... We imagine what else the women and men in a story might have thought, said or done... Many such stories were told by our ancestors to enrich the stories of the Bible.'

3 *Feather on the Breath of God: Sequences and Hymns* by Abbess Hildegard of Bingen. Cassette recording by 'Gothic Voices' directed by Christopher Page. © Hyperion Records Ltd., London, 1982.

 See also Flanagan, Sabina, *Hildegard of Bingen 1098–1179: A Visionary Life*, Routledge, 1989.

CHAPTER TWO

Shaping the story

Whatever the story, if it is carefully chosen and well prepared, it will give pleasure.

EILEEN COLWELL, *A STORYTELLER'S CHOICE*, P. 208.

Once a choice of story has been made, the next step is to shape and prepare to share the material. Perhaps the most demanding part of this process for the teller is simply to be able to remember the story. Even with familiar material, it takes focused preparation in order to be able reliably to recall and present a given selection. This section offers two good ways to approach this task:

❖ The three-line story skeleton
❖ The cartoon outline

Both these approaches work better than memorizing a script. They offer a patterned approach to claiming the material and identify signposts as *aides-mémoire* to accompany the actual telling. The *three-line story skeleton* constructs a short sentence outline which is easy to remember and easy to store. The *cartoon outline* creates a visual map using colour, shapes and symbols as a guide for remembering a story. The two approaches may appeal differently to individual tellers; one approach rather than another may be more appropriate to use with a given piece of material.

Both these techniques enable the teller to adapt a given piece of material in length and choice of vocabulary to accommodate the needs of different listening groups. The outlines developed are helpful for self-evaluation after an event. They can also serve as useful references as you collect a repertoire of tested material.

The three-line skeleton

What is it?

This is a method for identifying the main points of a story. Ordering these points in three short, clear sentences provides a framework around which more details may be added. The approach was developed some years ago while working with a small group of people who wanted to tell more stories in the course of preaching and teaching. Many have since found this approach useful in shaping stories from a variety of sources.

Creating the skeleton working with lived experience

Try it out for yourself. This part of the exercise should take you less than ten minutes to complete. We'll begin by working with a personal experience and apply the technique to working with a Bible story later in the chapter. You can work along as you read through this section. You might want something to write on as you go, but even that isn't strictly necessary. I'll work alongside and offer examples to illustrate the process.

To begin, **recollect something that has happened to you** that you would be willing to share. It could be a humorous event, something surprising or even scary. It might be an event where you remember that God was very much a part of what was happening, even if you might not have been so aware of it at the time.

Take time to recall the event as a whole. Begin at the beginning and follow what happened through to the end. If your remembering is visual, be aware of the scenes and the characters who carry out the actions. If your remembering is more of moods and feelings, notice how they change through the experience. Give yourself time to get the whole event in mind.

Now go back to the beginning. **Try to catch how or where this event started, in one short, clear sentence.** Make the sentence short and strong enough to remember easily, even though you might want to write it down. Remember that the opening sentence needs to attract people's attention, set the scene, and invite them into the story.

The event I've chosen to work with is an incident that occurred when I was helping to publicize our church fair. I was dressed as a clown, working with others who were distributing leaflets in the town centre. It wasn't the first time that 'Nibbles', my clown character, had appeared on the street.

My first sentence is: 'The clown walked down the street leading an imaginary dog.'

When you have chosen your first line, 'fast forward' your memory to the end of the event. How did the experience end? Try to summarize this moment in another short, strong sentence. **Make the last sentence as strong as the first.** This last sentence acts like a 'punch line' to bring the story to a definite close. Don't let the end of your story fade weakly away.

The last sentence from my experience is: 'The angry people who had gathered began to move away, laughing and smiling to each other.'

These two sentences provide clear foundations for retelling the story. Knowing the beginning and the end gives the teller control over travelling the distance between them.

Now move back to the midpoint of the story. This is the third critical reference point, or 'bone' in the three-line skeleton. It identifies the climax of the story—the point at which the energy changes, the twist in the tale happens. This is the unexpected event that determines how the experience will turn out. **Try to catch this moment in a third short, strong sentence.** Note that sometimes there are two significant moments, which make a 'four-line skeleton' a more effective model. For the purpose of this exercise, try to identify a single critical mid-point in the experience.

The third sentence, the mid-point, in my skeleton is: 'A small white poodle approached the dog on the "empty" lead and began to bark furiously.'

Now **rearrange the three sentences in their correct order** —beginning, middle, end. Read them all together. This outline provides the framework or 'bones' of your skeleton, upon which the details of the rest of the story may later be fleshed out.

My three-line skeleton reads:

The clown walked down the street leading an imaginary dog.
A small white poodle approached the dog on the 'empty' lead and began to bark furiously.
The angry people who had gathered began to move away, laughing and smiling to each other.

Obviously such an outline doesn't tell the whole story. Interesting details and other significant factors aren't included. None the less, the general frame of the story or experience should be clear. When developing this exercise in a group situation, this is the point at which I invite people to choose partners and *practise retelling the story from the skeleton*. If you're on your own right now, telling the story from the skeleton may not be so easy for you to try out.

Can you practise with an imaginary listener? If you're on your own, speak your story out loud. Give yourself about three minutes. Try to begin and end with the sentences you've selected and put the mid-point line in at the appropriate place. You can think it through quietly if you prefer, but hearing the sound of your voice and actually speaking out the words is a somewhat different experience.

When working in a group, people become very curious to hear the full story suggested by individual three-line skeletons. Since the purpose of the structure is to attract interest and hold attention, such curiosity is the mark of a measure of success. There is usually time for at least one or two people to tell their stories to the whole group.

Keeping in mind the fact that a story heard is very different from one read off a page, let me tell you the story behind the example in my skeleton.

Nibbles, my clown, was having a great time doing a 'Meet and Greet' walkabout to promote the church fair. It was fun to invite people to pet and play with my invisible pet pup 'Poochie' who was with me, on the end of a very visible lead. Some people were willing to play along, others pretended we were both invisible, and one or two got a bit rude.

The surprise came when a woman walking a small white poodle came toward us. When the poodle came up level with the collar at the end of the lead guiding my own (albeit invisible) pup, he became very agitated and began to bark furiously. The exchange between the poodle and the 'empty' lead was so heated that a crowd began to gather. People were jostling each other to see what was happening and a display rack of shoes on the pavement in front of a shop was knocked over. There were shoes and people and barking dogs everywhere. Things were really beginning to get out of hand.

The whole event turned from an ugly mess into all good fun when a butcher who worked in another shop came out on to the pavement. He had a large bone in each hand and offered a treat to both the dogs. He got a great laugh. Such an unexpected, playful response made everything seem all right. The owner of the white poodle picked up her dog, and I picked up pet pup 'Poochie'. Bystanders helped replace the shoes on the display rack. The angry people who had gathered began to move away, laughing and smiling to each other.

Evaluating the exercise

Looking at my example, you might notice that when writing this I have changed the first sentence. While I might be able to remember the start of the story with the first 'bone', when it came time to retell it to you something more specific seemed to be required. Sentences two and three remained in the story more nearly as I planned them. All the details could be added, in the way they really happened, around the framework offered by my skeleton.

As I was 'telling' the story, it seemed to me that there was really more than one critical point along the way. Do you think a fourth 'bone' might improve the shape of this skeleton? If I were to add one, it would probably have something to do with the entry of the butcher, and the real bones he contributed.

It is always important to reflect on the results of an exercise or a story sharing. Here are some questions which might help your personal evaluation of how this exercise works for you.

❖ Could I recall and retell my experience from the skeleton I created?

❖ Do my three sentences, repeated in their correct order, provide an adequate outline of the experience as a whole?

❖ Could this outline be shaped in the telling by the addition of details appropriate for the event?

❖ What changes could I make to these sentences to make the outline clearer or easier to remember?

❖ Would a fourth sentence added make the outline more useful as a working tool?

Working with a story 'written down'

Working with a story written down or material taken from a book is slightly different from working with personal experience. **Creating a three-line skeleton enables us to become very familiar with written material through working with the process.** We take the story 'inside' ourselves and it almost becomes part of us. Later, when we bring it out to share with others, some of our own authentic experience will surely come too.

The words and phrases which we use in the retelling may be different from what was written on the page, but the story we tell must be the same story. We may alter the setting, or even retell the story from the point of view of a different character in the story. None the less, **we as tellers are bound in truthfulness and respect not to pass on a different story from the one we have received.** Especially when working with material from our faith tradition, our fidelity must be to the truth of the tale itself.[1]

Another look at the skeleton shows how each of the lines in this approach has an important role to play in the shaping of the story as a whole. The *opening sentence* of a story told needs to both catch the attention of the listener and to focus it on what is about to happen. In order for it to be effective, and for the teller to be able to remember it, the sentence must be short and clear as well as interesting.

The *last sentence* in the outline acts like a punch line. Its function is to collect the whole experience of the story in one summarizing image. This image holds the point of the story for the listener and constitutes the teller's last word. If the beginning of the story is important to get people's attention, the end of the story is equally important for bringing the sharing to a definite and memorable close.

We have lots of practice in getting people's attention with what we say but much less experience in bringing what we say to closure. In conversation, very often someone else has already intervened and diverted attention before we completely finish speaking. In the same way, another speaker might have added an idea to a point we were developing or even changed the flow of the conversation before we reached any sort of conclusion. In the practice of storytelling, there is no one else to bring the story to a close. An unprepared end which simply trails away is unfaithful to the story received and unsatisfying to the listener.

The *second line* in the skeleton locates the moment in the story when something happens to make the story take a different turn from what was initially expected. The purpose of creating this midpoint sentence last is to give the teller a clear sense that the goal of the telling is to get to the end. The climax of the story is only a staging point along the way. When fleshing out the details of the story in the telling, this point can be very important to the teller. It is easy enough to get distracted in the retelling and perhaps add too much detail. Without such a clear midpoint to provide direction and an endpoint to offer focus, the aim of the telling could be lost. Even worse, the attention of the listener can also be lost.

Working with a story from the Bible

The three-line skeleton is also effective for preparing biblical material for retelling. A retelling rather than a rereading might make a very appropriate contribution to the Ministry of the Word in parish worship. Such a retelling might also be geared for work with younger children in Junior Church.

To carry on with this part of the exercise, select a Bible story with which you would like to work. Trust yourself to choose a passage that attracts you at the moment. Once again I'll work alongside and offer an example of the process. Once you've chosen the passage, read it through to the end. If it's a Gospel story and appears in more than one place, it is useful to read through each one.

I will work with the reports of the baptism of Jesus. Some account of this event appears in all four Gospels.[2] I will draw my three-line skeleton primarily from the text in Matthew.

In those days John the Baptist appeared in the wilderness of Judea, proclaiming, 'Repent, for the kingdom of heaven has come near.' This is the one of whom the prophet Isaiah spoke when he said, 'The voice of one crying in the wilderness: Prepare the way of the Lord, make his paths straight.'

Now John wore clothing of camel's hair and a leather belt around his waist, and his food was locusts and wild honey. Then the people of Jerusalem and all Judea were going out to him, and all the region along the Jordan, and they were baptized by him in the river Jordan, confessing their sins (Matthew 3:1–6).

Then Jesus came from Galilee to John at the Jordan, to be baptized by him. John would have prevented him, saying, 'I need to be baptized by you, and do you come to me?' But Jesus answered him. 'Let it be so now; for it is proper for us in this way to fulfil all righteousness.' Then he consented. And when Jesus had been baptized, just as he came up from the water, suddenly the heavens were opened to him and he saw the Spirit of God descending like a dove, and alighting on him. And a voice from heaven said, 'This is my Son, the Beloved, with whom I am well pleased' (3:13–17).

Having read through the passage as a whole, go back to the beginning. Draw out an opening sentence that is short and clear.

Perhaps an example might be:

'John was living in the desert, baptizing people by the river Jordan.'

Now 'fast forward' to the end of your passage. Make the last sentence for your skeleton equally strong. The last line from this example might be:

'Some thought they heard God say, "This is my Son and I love him."'

Thirdly, choose a midpoint sentence. Remember that this is really a climactic moment, a point in the event when something happens upon which the rest of the story turns. The midpoint from this story might be:

'Jesus was baptized by John.'

Finally, rearrange the sentences in the correct order. Put the 'bones' in place in the skeleton and see how they read. Does the storyline come clear when you say them out in the correct order? Here are the 'bones' from the Matthew passage.

John was living in the desert, baptizing people by the river Jordan.

Jesus was baptized by John.

Some thought they heard God say, 'This is my Son and I love him.'

Now try to retell the story from this skeleton. Are the sentences short and strong enough for you to remember them without the page of notes in front of you? Try it. Give yourself about three minutes for this first attempt.

If you're alone, you will probably find your 'invisible' listening partner very receptive. Even better, try it out on a friend. Remember, stories tell differently than they 'read', and the listener is as significant a part of the experience as the teller and the tale itself.

Were you successful? It is always important to reflect on the process you have just explored and to draw profit from what you have experienced. Here are some points which might guide your reflection.

❖ Could I retell the story using the sentences from my skeleton?
❖ Did the sentences give the shape of the whole event?
❖ Was I able to stick to the time?
❖ Would it be possible to expand the telling from the skeleton?
❖ If I were to tell this story again, what additions or changes would I make?

Before moving on to the next exercise, read through the biblical text(s) again. Notice this time particularly the additional details which are included and perhaps told from different points of view in different texts. This textual material is relevant to the shaping of your telling and retelling.

Look again at how the story of the baptism of Jesus is presented in each of the four Gospels. Notice that the Gospel accounts themselves are very carefully constructed. According to the event for which you might be retelling this passage, might one of the other Gospels offer you more relevant details? Do you know where additional details and background information may be found to flesh out the 'skeletons' they present?

One strength of the *three-line skeleton* is that it may be stored and recalled should you want to tell the story again. Keeping track of the stories you prepare for telling helps to extend your repertoire and build your own confidence as a teller. Notes and annotations recorded after a telling also help for future applications. At the time, the experience is so present with us that it seems we'll never forget, yet over time significant learning and relevant insights can be lost. Even brief notes and one or two reflective comments written in a journal or stored somewhere alongside the skeleton can trigger useful information for repeated applications.

The cartoon outline

Wherever you turn your eyes, there is God's symbol,
Whatever you read, there you will find God's types.[3]

Here is another technique for helping to remember a story. The aim is to create a picture or cartoon outline using colour, figures and simple shapes. This cartoon outline can be a helpful guide while practising the story and can be used later as a prompt if you are concerned about omitting significant detail. With words and phrases added to it, this out-line can be filed for reference and used to help you build and remember, perhaps, the more complicated stories you wish to tell.

This pattern of preparation works well with stories which include a series of events that happen in a specific order. I have found that the story of creation (Genesis 1—2:3) and the parable of the sower (Mark 4:1–9) are two Bible stories which can usefully be prepared by working with this method. Creating a cartoon outline is also effective preparation for helping to turn personal experience into story. Even familiar material can include details whose order can become easily confused. Not only can the cartoon outline help in the preparation of the story, it can also suggest ideas for visual aids and group participation which may be added later to enhance the presentation.

Assemble and prepare the materials

You might want to collect a few materials so that you can work along as you read through this exercise. Don't be afraid to continue, *especially* if you've never received good marks for drawing ability. This is a 'for your eyes only' document and is designed to create visual clues to support your own preparation process. You will need:
❖ something to write/draw on, preferably a plain sheet of A4 paper
❖ a Bible
❖ a selection of coloured markers, pens, or crayons

For this exercise, the story of creation (Genesis 1—2:3) will serve as a working example. It is a long text so I recommend that you find it and read it alongside the extracts included here. It may also be interesting to notice how the interpretative phrases used in different versions of the Bible relate to each other.

You need to prepare the paper to use. Hold the piece of paper open in front of you. Fold it in half—lengthways. Now fold that long strip in half, and fold it in half again. When you reopen the paper, you should see eight equal sections (four in each row). Lay the unfolded paper in front of you—lengthways—with boxes from 1 to 4 across the top row, and boxes 5 to 8 along the second row. The plan is to enter in each box a shape or image or shades of colour... or some of all three... to serve as a reminder for what happened in each 'day' of creation. With eight boxes and seven 'days' of creation, you have one spare box to use, or not, as you go through the exercise.

When you have the materials assembled, pause for a moment. Take a deep breath and release it. Clear your mind of other concerns. Allow your whole mind and heart, your thoughtfulness and creativity to be available for what you are about to do.

Create the cartoon outline

When you are ready to continue, **read through the entire passage** to remind yourself of the story. Take the time you need, but plan to read the passage from beginning to end in order to catch the story as a whole.

Now return to the beginning of the selection and **re-read the 'first day'** more closely. Notice the shapes and images that suggest themselves as you read; be aware of moods or feelings that might be more easily expressed in colour.

In the beginning when God created the heavens and the earth, the earth was a formless void and darkness covered the face of the deep, while a wind from God swept over the face of the waters. Then God said, 'Let there be light'; and there was light. And God saw that the light was good; and God separated the light from the darkness. God called the light Day, and the darkness he called Night. And there was evening and there was morning, the first day (Genesis 1:1–5).

In the first box, sketch a shape or symbol which will remind you of the beginning of the story—perhaps making use of colour. You might like to use up the extra box at this point (taking one for 'In the beginning' and another for the 'first day'); alternatively you might choose to keep the extra box for later use. (God was *very* busy on the third day!) Since you know that there are seven days to be created and eight boxes to do it in, there is a bit of space for your own creativity.

Give yourself permission to respond playfully: remember that this is for your eyes only, not a piece of work to be put on display or graded for drawing ability! A word or phrase may be helpful but keep in mind that the goal of this technique is to create a visual aid to memory.

Now **move on to the 'second day'**. Read the next bit of the text, remembering to still your mind and to focus your attention on the 'day' you encounter.

And God said, 'Let there be a dome in the midst of the waters, and let it separate the waters from the waters.' So God made the dome and separated the waters that were under the dome from the waters that were above the dome. And it was so. God called the dome Sky. And there was evening and there was morning, the second day (Genesis 1:6–8).

What picture will hold this division for you? Don't labour too long over your response; try to catch your strongest idea. You can adjust any of the boxes later if you have a better idea.

When you are ready, **move on to the 'third day'**.

And God said, 'Let the waters under the sky be gathered together into one place, and let the dry land appear.' And it was so. God called the dry land Earth, and the waters that were gathered together he called Seas. And God saw that it was good. Then God said, 'Let the earth put forth vegetation: plants yielding seed, and fruit trees of every kind on earth that bear fruit with the seed in it.' And it was so. The earth brought forth vegetation: plants yielding seed of every kind, and trees of every kind bearing fruit with the seed in it. And God saw that it was good. And there was evening and there was morning, the third day (Genesis 1:9–13).

This 'day' of creation may require a bit more space. As I read through this part of the passage, I was surprised at how much happened on the third day. I still wonder at the new insights which present themselves when working with biblical material; no matter how familiar the passage, there always seems to be something more to discover.

When you have found a satisfactory way to catch the appearance of both the dry land and the whole cycle of vegetation, move on to the 'fourth day'.

Continue in a similar fashion until six days of creation are accomplished. Keep in mind that while key words and phrases are helpful, discovering visual clues as tools to remembering the development of a narrative is the focus of this exercise.

Day seven

Thus the heavens and the earth were finished, and all their multitude. And on the seventh day God finished the work that he had done, and he rested on the seventh day from all the work that he had done. So God blessed the seventh day and hallowed it, because on it God rested from all the work that he had done in creation (Genesis 2:1–3).

By the time you've completed the 'seventh day', perhaps you'll be ready for a rest as well. Allow yourself a bit of applause for completing the task and then take a stretch break. As you do, I invite you to be aware of the thoughts and feelings that you experienced as you were working through the passage. While more difficult to express in pictures or even in words, these thoughts and feelings provide useful background for your own retelling.

Part of what attracts and holds the attention of the listener, and enlivens the tale itself, is the communication of the authentic experience of the teller. The remembrance of your own inner feelings while working through even this expression of creation will provide a useful experience to draw on.

Telling the story

Now look over the cartoon you've completed. Can you follow the whole story through from beginning to end with your cartoon outline? Do you need to add a word or two in one box or another to keep yourself on track? Prepare to tell the story from this outline.

Working in a group is an advantage at this point, because it is possible to share with one another. Ask a friend or family member to listen to your run-through. If you are alone, your imaginary listener may be invited back into the scene. However you manage the space, take the time to tell the story out loud. It makes a difference actually to speak out the words.

Don't labour too hard over the choice of words in this first trial run. Allow yourself to use very simple language and short phrases. It is most important at this point to be able simply to work through the story from beginning to end.

When you have told the story once, give yourself a pat on the back. Well done! You deserve a rest... remember the seventh day!

When you've had a bit of a break, take time to reflect on what you have done and then try it again. Here are some questions that might help you to consider and possibly adjust the retelling.

- ❖ Can you recognize the details and order presented in the narrative?
- ❖ Do the key words you've chosen help to move from one event to another?
- ❖ Do your own sketches suggest ideas for larger cards or tangible objects which could be used to help you, the teller, as well as the listeners, to move through the story?

Practise telling and retelling this story from the cartoon. Storytelling is fun, we all can do it, and it is important to take time to prepare the stories well.

NOTES

1 Nicholas Lash discusses this understanding and concept in Lash, N., 'Performing the Scriptures', *Theology on the Road to Emmaus*.

2 Matthew 3:1–6, 11–17; Mark 1:4–11; Luke 3:2–3, 21–22; John 1:6–8, 23, 28–34.

3 Brock, S., *The Luminous Eye: The Spiritual World Vision of St Ephraim*, a CIIS Publication, Rome, 1985, p. 27.

∞

CHAPTER THREE

Stepping into the story

...Sunlight dances.

My spirit,
Stirring with the shifting tide,
Takes up the journey.

ANN LEWIN, 'TIDE TURN', *CANDLES AND KINGFISHERS*, P. 89.

Storytelling involves the whole of us—body, mind and spirit. Movement and body language are as important to a well-prepared story as the choice of words and images. This exercise will focus on the physical aspects of preparing a piece of material well. It is based on the understanding that paying attention to the physical expression of our thoughts and feelings can stimulate fresh insight and deepen our understanding. This exercise provides an opportunity:

❖ to explore the movement and body language which might relate to a given story

❖ to develop ways to integrate relevant insights into the telling of the story

'Stepping into the story' is a physical and imaginative approach to the exploration of Bible stories. It has developed from an exercise led by Margie Brown during a series of workshops at The Pacific Coast School of Theology, Berkeley, California.

This exercise has proved useful to individuals in the preparation of biblical material for telling. It can be adapted for presentation with even quite large groups. 'Stepping into the story' has also proved effective in establishing points for conversation and sharing within all-age groups.

Introduction: for yourself

Choose a story

Choose a story that you are happy to work with: an incident from one of the Gospel stories of the life and ministry of Jesus seems to work well with this exercise. For illustration, I will work with the incident where Jesus meets Zacchaeus (Luke 19:1–10). Find your own passage in the Bible and read it through to reacquaint yourself with the story-line.

When you have the story once more in mind, set the book aside. The object of this exercise is to literally 'step into the story'. The aim is not to prepare a dramatic skit as such, but rather to explore the story with movement. We can draw clues and ideas for retelling the story from the way our body moves and from the thoughts and feelings that come as we move through the story.

Choose a space

Choose a space in which you can move in the room where you are working. Stand up and do some gentle stretching. Reach up and out with your arms. Lift and release your shoulders once or twice. Lean your head gently from side to side. Move up and down on tiptoes. Stand first on one foot and then the other; bend and move the suspended leg gently. Flex and extend each foot, rotating it in both directions at the ankle. Take one or two deep breaths and exhale slowly. Wiggle your hips and bottom and give a bit of an all-over shake. Feel your body ready to go ahead.

Move through the story

Partially close your eyes. Even though you are alone in the room, you may find this helps your concentration. You will still be able to see enough to avoid bumping into things. When you are ready to continue, bring to mind the story you have chosen. As you follow the story-line from beginning to end, act out or take the position of all the *nouns* in the story. Sometimes I say, try to 'become' the objects in the story... not the people, but the things. For instance, in my example the story begins:

Jesus entered Jericho and was passing through it (on the way to Jerusalem to celebrate the Passover). A man was there named Zacchaeus; he was a chief tax collector and was rich. He was trying to see who Jesus was, but on account of the crowd he could not, because he was short in stature. So he ran ahead and climbed a sycamore tree to see him, for Jesus was going to pass that way (Luke 19:1–4).

As you try to take the position of the nouns, you might lie down and actually become the road Jesus walked on, then step into a position as the tree Zacchaeus climbed. As you continue moving through to the end of the story, you might form the house Zacchaeus lived in... the roof, the walls... perhaps even the table at which he sat with Jesus.

Remember that this movement is not intended for public performance; the exercise is offered as one possible way to stimulate ideas in your personal preparation.

Now open your eyes to get your bearings. Go back to the beginning of the story and prepare to move through the story again. As you move through the story a second time, act out all the *verbs* in the story: 'do' the action words. 'Doing' the action words in the beginning of the Zacchaeus story might include walking, running, climbing. As you continue to the end of the story, what actions would follow?

When Jesus came to the place, he looked up and said to him, 'Zacchaeus, hurry and come down; for I must stay at your house today.' So he hurried down, and was happy to welcome him (Luke 19:5–6).

When you have come to the end of the story, open your eyes and take your bearings once more. Prepare to move through the story for a third and final time. This time, *take the position of one of the characters in the story.* Perhaps you might walk through the story as Jesus, using appropriate bearing, movement and gestures. Perhaps you would be Zacchaeus, stepping into his size and expressions of curiosity, longing and desire. Perhaps you might be a member of the crowd. The crowd is there from the beginning and important for the climax of the story:

All (the people in the crowd) who saw it began to grumble and said, 'He has gone to be the guest of one who is a sinner.' Zacchaeus stood there and said to the Lord, 'Look, half of my possessions, Lord, I will give to the poor; and if I have defrauded anyone of anything, I will pay back four times as much.' Then Jesus said to him, 'Today salvation has come to this house, because he too is a son of Abraham. For the Son of Man came to seek out and to save the lost' (Luke 19:7–10).

As you walk through in your character's place, do not try to come up with dialogue at this point; rather concentrate on a physical interpretation of the different characters.

Repeat the process

You might choose to walk through more than once to explore the experience of different characters. Perhaps you might speculate on the position of other members of the community who might have been there but are not mentioned in the story. For instance, would Zacchaeus have had a wife, or servants? What about the disciples of Jesus, and the women who travelled with them? What might their positions and movements in the story have been like?

Reflect on what you've experienced

Take a few minutes to reflect on the work you have just completed.
❖ How did it feel to enter the story in this way?
❖ What insights did you receive?
❖ Were there any surprises?

❖ If you were to retell that story as a first-person account from the point of view of one of the characters, whom would you choose?

Retell the story

The culminating activity of this exercise is to retell in your own words the story you have chosen. Draw on the movement you have worked through to help set the scene. Allow the narrative to come alive from the point of view of one of the characters. While the preparation for the telling is done on your own, the story doesn't truly come alive until it is shared with a listener. Before sharing the story in a larger group, try it out with a friend or family member.

An adaptation: good for groups

Aims

This exercise has proved effective in work with groups of various sizes and objectives. The aim remains the same—to employ physical movement in the preparation of story material for retelling. In addition it has also proved able:

❖ to deepen trust and promote communication within a group
❖ to provide starting points for further developing the telling of individual faith stories
❖ to offer natural opportunities for sharing across the generations in all-age and family groups

Invite the group

Begin by drawing the group together in a circle. When introductions and initial sharing have been completed, present the aim of the exercise. Invite the members of the group to let their minds wander over the Bible stories they know, and to select one with which they might enjoy working.

Allow sufficient time for individuals to make a choice, to find the story in the Bible, and then to read through the story in order to be familiar with its shape and details. It is usually helpful to have biblical references for several stories written down and available, should individuals find it easier to make a choice from a suggested list.

When the group seems ready to proceed, lead the group in a simple series of stretches and warm-up exercises. Step into the middle of the room yourself. Invite the group members to put things out of their hands and to claim a space in the room where they can move around a bit. Be sure to acknowledge the needs of those members of the group who will prefer to do this work while sitting.

The pattern of the exercise is to invite the individuals to move through their chosen story several times. In order that each may have some privacy to do the work, ask them to close their eyes. It is as if a curtain is coming down around each one of them so each is free to explore their own ideas privately... behind drawn curtains, as it were.

Start the exercise

Say that you, the leader, will keep your eyes open to make sure no one runs into anyone else or bumps into a wall. Ask them to try it out. Your dialogue might be something like this:

Close your eyes and move around in your space a bit to see how it feels. Now open your eyes.

When I ask you to close your eyes again, or to 'bring down the curtain', start at the beginning of the story you have chosen and move through the action to the end of the story. Act out each of the main nouns—the naming words—in the story as you go along. If the story begins near a tree, or a well, if there is a table or a bed in the story, actually take the position of that object or place.

Move through the story, acting out the different nouns as you go. Use as much of your body and move as freely in your space as you are able. When you come to the end of your story, stand or sit still so that I will know when it's time to move along. When you are all finished, I will ask you to open your eyes and then give the next set of directions.

Watch the group so that individuals don't bump into each other or the walls. Allow enough time for them to move through their actions. When most seem to have finished, announce that it is time to bring their movement to an end. When all are still, ask them to open their eyes and re-establish their bearings. Your dialogue might continue like this:

That was the first time through. There will be two further opportunities to move through the story. This time the invitation will be to move through the story, acting out all the verbs—actually 'doing' the action words. Notice where Jesus and his friends are walking or running. Perhaps they are laughing or talking. Maybe it is raining; the fruit could be growing; and so on.

Now close your eyes, 'bring down the curtains', and begin again to move through the story. This time, act out all the 'doing' words. When you reach the end of the action, stand or sit still so that I will know when it is time to move on.

This is perhaps the part of the exercise where your watchful eye is most useful. Most people have a sense of their own safe space, even with eyes closed. None the less, you may need to move closer to gently intervene in order to forestall collisions. Usually drawing alongside the individual is enough to re-establish a sense of boundary without interrupting the flow of the work.

When most people seem finished, invite them all to bring their work to a close. When they are all still, invite them to open their eyes. The pattern of the work continues. For the third time through, the intent is to move through the story as one of the characters. Assume the stature and manner of the character. Use gestures, posture and movement to participate in their actions and interaction with others; save language and sound to be added at a later stage.

Continue the pattern of the dialogue as with the other two examples, suggesting that they limit their actions to the point of view of just one of the characters. Some people enjoy taking the position of Jesus; others find new insights from crossing gender lines. In the story of the holy family's journey to Bethlehem, people sometimes take the donkey's space. On one occasion, a 'chairbound' individual was able to participate by taking the role of the well near which Jesus sat to speak to a woman.

Close the exercise

When all seem to be finished, ask them to bring their work to a close and to 'open the curtains' for the last time. Even while people are still in their places, you can begin a reflective process with a series of questions asked of the whole group.

❖ Did you enjoy the experience?
❖ Which bit did you find most difficult?
❖ Did you experience something which you didn't expect to happen?

This isn't the time to invite lengthy answers, but accept or acknowledge any responses that individuals care to make at the time.

Reflect and share

The reflective/sharing space which follows is very important. Ask the members of the group now to choose a partner or to work in threes, if necessary. Tell them that they will have the next period of time to share between themselves, in order to tell each other the stories with which they were just working. Twenty minutes is a good length of time to offer the pairs.

Suggest that they make as much use of the available space as they are able, in order to find some private places where they may speak up or move around in some privacy and without being a disturbance to another pair. When pairs have been chosen, agree the time when the group will reconvene. Keep track of where the partners go to do their work in case you need to remind them near the time that it's almost time to return to the group.

When the group reconvenes, allow time for the pairs to share with the group any reflections they have about the exercise just completed. These comments to the group about what bits were difficult and what worked well allow the pairs to release necessary feelings. These comments also offer you, the leader, some useful feedback about the session and suggestions for possible future work.

Tell the story

It is very good practice to offer at least some individuals, if not each member of the group, an opportunity to share their story with a larger group. Depending on the size of the group and the timing schedule of the workshop, plan to have a sharing time after a good break or a general 'performance' space before the end of the whole event. It is important to balance periods of individual and group sharing with adequate break time and opportunities for private space. Most people can make very good use of sharing time when appropriate spaces for private reflection are also available.

∽

CHAPTER FOUR

Bag of Bags and the stories inside

'I must seek the treasure I've seen in my dream!'
'Then go with my blessing,' she said.
So placing what was needed in a good sized bag,
he set off on the road to Krakov.

FROM A RETELLING OF 'THE PEDDLER OF KRAKOV'.

The *Bag of Bags* is a resource tool that has varied applications in the development of the storyteller. It is a good visual resource for the individual and has proved very effective for working with groups. The Bag of Bags is particularly helpful for:

❖ extending the individual's ability to draw out stories from simple objects
❖ stimulating individual creativity
❖ converting personal experience into tellable story
❖ integrating individual experience into a larger tale

The sections in this chapter aim to:

❖ describe the creation of the Bag of Bags
❖ offer a step-by-step plan for using it with a group

- share a story application appropriate for an all-age group
- suggest connections for telling Bible stories

The story of the Bag of Bags itself

Why it began

In response to my need to find new ways to encourage people to become familiar with finding 'stories, stories everywhere', artist Pauline Vincent offered me a 'Bag of Bags'. She had created this wonderfully flexible resource for her own use to foster Early Years learning. It is basically one large bag, within which are additional bags of various sizes. Each of the inner bags is itself unique.

The individual bags are made in different sizes of various fabrics, so each one looks and feels quite distinctive. They are constructed differently so they open and close and are held together in various ways, for example by zippers, cords, buttons, Velcro, and so on. They are of different shapes, some dramatically unique in the form of interesting creatures, others designed to fold and unfold unexpectedly, others quite straightforward and simple in design.

The look and feel of it

Each of the inner bags contains two or three objects. These objects are very simple things which somehow seem to 'fit' with the shape, size, and feel of the bag itself. For example, a zippered bag of printed calico contains a spool of thread, a small pair of scissors, and several lengths of coloured ribbon. A folded length of rough burlap holds a pocket knife, a multi-faceted glistening stone, and the stump of a candle.

Other bags contain individual beads, pieces of mirror, small boxes, bits of driftwood, lengths of cord, and so on. One large fabric drawstring bag opens to release a long-tailed, long-limbed furry monkey which calls out for mischief as a hand-puppet.

Additions and replacements

Over time, my inner bags and their contents have been changed around, or unexpectedly disappeared, and others have been added to accommodate larger or smaller groups. In fact, the original bag itself and all its contents needed to be replaced when it was sadly lost 'in transit'. I've often wondered what happened when the new owner opened it at leisure... perhaps the unexpected contents would be recognized as treasures, perhaps not.

Repetitions

The experience of loss did teach me, however, that such a resource can be collected from ordinary situations—the back of a drawer, the bottom of the closet, the local charity shop, a bric-a-brac stall at the church fair, or odds and ends from a car boot sale. New ideas for inner bags often present themselves. One of the current collection looks ever so much like a sock, tied round with a shoelace.

You can collect a similar resource. My experience suggests that it is well the worth the time it takes. Begin with the small bags you might find in your own drawers and closets. A sponge bag, a pencil case, even the carrying case for an all-weather mac might suggest starting points. Small fabric bags that once held bath beads, or pot pourri, or a spare pair of spectacles, might be other possibilities. Let your imagination loose. There's no telling where it might take you. Stories and the resources with which to trigger the telling of them really can be found everywhere.

Your growing collection might be stored at first in a backpack, or a sports bag, or even the string bag in which you once carried your school gym kit. When your Bag of Bags contains even a small collection of inner bags, you can experiment with releasing the stories inside. The following pattern is designed for interactive, adult groups but is also adaptable for use with different age groups.

The stories inside the Bag of Bags

Introducing the exercise

First, invite the group to form a circle; bring chairs or sit on the floor. It is important to establish a rapport which will give people permission to experiment—to play with the material.

Once the group is settled, focused and ready to continue, place the Bag of Bags in the centre of the circle. Leave it unopened, in full view, while inviting the group to consider that the contents of the bag consist of materials with which to tell many stories. Go on to explain that the purpose of this exercise will be to unpack and explore the stories suggested by the materials inside. It will be an opportunity to integrate imagination and lived experience.

Unpacking the Bag of Bags

Move back into the middle of the circle and have a good look at the bag before opening it. Turn it over and around. If there are outside straps or pockets, investigate each one before moving on to look inside the bag itself. Now deliberately undo the fastening of the Bag of Bags. Looking inside, begin carefully to remove the individual bags. Lay them out on the floor, one at a time. It's not necessary to make many comments at this point. If you are focusing your own attention on the unpacking process, the attention of the group will be focused there also.

Making a choice

When all the inner bags are displayed in the circle, return to your own seat. Allow a minute or two for everyone to have a good look at the whole collection. When the time seems right, invite everyone in the circle to select a bag and return with it unopened to their place. The group dynamics at this point are very interesting: making the choice, for some people, is quite tough. It is helpful to suggest that it might be necessary to take a second choice in case someone else got to their favourite one first. Sometimes it's also helpful, before moving on, to offer people an opportunity to swap for any of the remaining bags.

Continue with the directions by asking people to really explore the bag they've chosen, before opening it. How does it look? What is special about the appearance? What kind of fabric is it made of? How does it feel? Is the material soft... stiff... scratchy? Does it have a special smell? Does the smell have to do with the bag itself, or what's inside? How is it fastened? Does it open and close in a simple or a complicated manner? Do they have any idea about what the bag might contain?

Once the senses have been fully employed in the exploration of the bag, suggest that the bags may now be opened. What do the bags contain? People may take out each of the objects inside and explore them as carefully as they explored the bag. Ask the group to consider: 'What do you notice especially about each object? What memories or thoughts come up for you as you handle them?' Encourage them to be aware of any feelings that the objects evoke.

Claiming the story

The next step in the exercise is to claim the story that might be told by integrating each of the objects and the bag itself. To stimulate the imagination, ask the group what sort of person might have chosen each of these objects and put them in the bag? What clues do they give about the age, gender, interests, or home territory of the individual? What might the occupation of such an individual be?

The story can be extended by considering why these objects might have been collected and saved. Do they seem to come from modern times or from times past? Are they of local origin or have they come from foreign lands? Would they have been commemorating a festive occasion or perhaps even a sad happening?

Allow the imagining process to continue. Can the group make any potential connections between this developing scenario and their own experiences? Might this be something one of their friends or family might have done? Could the person have been related to them, or perhaps the ancestor of a friend? Is there a story developing that might be an incident in a family's history or even in the imagined background of an organization or group of friends?

Allow some time for ideas to develop, but not to become laboured. Keep in mind that this is a spontaneous, imaginative exercise designed to stimulate stories for sharing. The process of telling the stories is the focus of the exercise. In an exercise timed to last approximately 45 to 50 minutes, the whole process thus far might be timed to take 15 to 20 minutes.

Shaping the story

So far we've been considering the story that might be stimulated by such a collection of objects. Having claimed the story, the next step is to give it a shape in which it can later be shared and perhaps retold. Stories are composed of a beginning, a middle and an end. The beginning of the story needs to attract the attention of the listener and to set the character, place, and time of the story.

Beginning

Encourage the group members to think: **'How would you begin the story that might be told from the bag you've chosen?'** Would you ask a question or point out something about the bag itself? Would you establish a personal connection, perhaps saying something like, 'One of my ancestors was in the merchant navy...' or 'My friend Mary's grandmother was in service with...'? Or would you begin with a phrase like 'Once upon a time...' or 'There once was...'?

Middle

The objects taken out of the bag are the clues to the middle part of the story. Ask your group to select three ideas or strong points from their imagined scenario that will be interesting. Although they may add or subtract other details as the story develops in the telling, these points will help to give the story a shape. If there are only three or four minutes to tell the story, it is important to keep the shape simple and clear in the mind. The objects themselves may help individuals to remember the details they want to include.

End

How will the story end? It is important to have a strong finish. The listener needs to be clear that the teller has finished. With a descriptive narrative, as this story is likely to be, drawing the details to a considered conclusion is important. It may be that questions are raised which do not have answers; none the less, details are best not left unacknowledged. A twist in the tale, an unexpected connection which brings the story to a close helps make it memorable. A question which connects the events of the story to the listener's own experience can also be a successful ending.

Group members are now ready to review their story as a whole. Sometimes having worked through to the end, a different beginning suggests itself. Are they happy now with the shape they've chosen?

Provide time for people to go through their stories again to themselves, letting the objects themselves help to move through the story in the telling.

Sharing the story

Divide up into pairs or threesomes. Allow eight to ten minutes for individuals to tell each other the story of the bag each one chose. Refer again to the significance of the listener in the process. Encourage the listeners to try to catch the story as a whole as well as to notice one or two points of feedback which may be offered to the teller in response. Before returning to the whole group circle, allow some time for individuals to reflect on the stories shared and to share responses.

As the small groups are invited to return to the large circle, so must the individual bags be returned to the Bag of Bags itself. To bring the exercise to closure, place the Bag of Bags in the centre of the circle again. Invite individuals to come, in the order that seems appropriate, to replace the individual bags. Sometimes returning the bags is accompanied by strong feelings as people can identify quite intimately with the story they've discovered in the bag.

Suggest that individuals say as much, or as little, as they like about the story that came out of their work with this particular bag. Some may also find it helpful to articulate why they chose a particular bag and how they feel about returning it. Perhaps there will be some who would prefer not to share with a large group. I have found that, more often than not, many would like to retell their story as a whole. The size of the group and the length of time already shared may determine the possibility of this.

Further reflection
Here are some questions which may help to collect and deepen the learnings from this exercise.
- ❖ What worked particularly well for me in this exercise?
- ❖ Where did the exercise seem difficult or unhelpful?
- ❖ Are there any elements which might be applicable to my own story preparation and presentations?
- ❖ Could this exercise be usefully adapted for the situations or groups to which I contribute?

These questions are useful for individual reflection as well as for group consideration. It may also be helpful, as part of the exercise, to schedule a period of time for small groups to reflect together on the strengths and weaknesses of the exercise, and to identify personal learnings which have developed through the work.

An application: an imagined tale

The story begins
This story developed during a storytelling workshop some years ago. It has served as a framework for presenting an application of the Bag of Bags. It follows a pattern of presentation which introduces a 'story within a story' and allows individual work to be integrated into received material. This application may serve as a model for developing other similar interweaving of parallel stories and personal experience. It has proved effective with adult groups, with children in schools and library programmes, and for enabling sharing in all-age groups.

Once, long ago, there was a land ruled by a king and queen. They were good monarchs and the land flourished under their leadership. There was no want and people lived together in peace and harmony. The king and queen were as good for each other as they were for their people. They shared their joys and sorrows and worked together to rule. On the day of their wedding, the king and queen received a gift which was at the heart of the prosperity of the land.

The gift was a crystal box. It was wonderfully made, of a good size. The double doors swung open from the middle; it was very easy to reach inside. The crystal box sat in the middle of the throne room from the time it was presented. It remained available to all who came to receive from it.

The box had special properties. It could supply the needs and desires of all who approached it. One had only to stand before the box, ask for what was needed, and then reach inside to receive the request. The only requirement was that when one gift was removed from the box, something else was put back in return.

Daily the people of the land came through the throne room. Everyone's needs and desires were fulfilled. There was enough to eat and attractive clothing to wear. There were toys for the children to play with and all manner of things with which to amuse the adults. People were careful to replace one gift with another; there was plenty for all. There was little sickness or crime… the doors of the throne room were open to all. People lived a long and full life.

During all this time, three thieves lived at the edge of the land. They were unemployed. They had never had cause to practise their craft. None the less, they often met and one day they began to make plans to steal the crystal box. Taking it out of the palace would be no problem. The doors of the throne room were always open, even as everyone slept. Finding a place to hide the box occupied them mostly.

One day, they came across a very remote cave with a small but adequate entrance, a dry flat floor, and a high domed ceiling. With this as a secure hiding-place, they vowed to act quickly.

The very next night, the three approached the throne room and, finding it empty, drew close to the crystal box. Two of them secured the central doors, lifted it clear of its resting-place, and moved across the room carrying it between them. The third thief went ahead to make sure no one would interrupt their progress. All through the night they travelled; morning found them approaching their hideout.

Setting the crystal box in the middle of the domed cave, the three prepared to satisfy their cravings, uninterrupted. 'A bag of gold!' called out the first thief. A bag of gold was drawn out of the box and the thief moved across the cave to set it down away from the others. Not wanting even now to be outdone, the second thief also called out, 'A bag of gold!' The second thief also established a 'stash' away from the other two. Needing to be like the others, even though this wasn't what was intended, the third thief also called out, 'A bag of gold!' and found a place for the stash, as separate as it could be.

Then the first thief returned to the box: 'A bag of gold!' 'Bag of gold!' called the second thief, and the third thief claimed the same. 'Bag of gold!' 'Bag of gold!' 'Bag of gold!' Time after time the thieves drew out these bags of treasure and piled them jealously in their own corners. Higher and higher grew their piles, wider and wider, until nearly the whole floor space was ringed with bags of gold. Still they drew treasure from the box and pushed the bags higher and nearer to the domed point of the ceiling of the cave.

'Bag of gold!' 'Bag of gold!' 'Bag of gold!' They had hardly paused for breath. Surely they had neither eaten nor left the cave, fearing to fall behind in the accumulation of treasure. 'Bag of gold!' 'Bag of gold!' 'Bag of...'. Straining and pushing, the third thief struggled to stack the latest withdrawal from the box and then, all of a sudden, the whole edifice collapsed... inward... burying the thieves and crushing the crystal box.

As soon as the box was broken, a great wound opened in the earth and bags and bones alike were sucked into the depths of the hole. All that was left when all was still again were shards of glass in the middle of the room and one or two solitary bags of gold remaining at the edge of the cave.

While the thieves had been claiming the gold, the king and queen awoke to discover the loss of the box in the throne room.

Startled and saddened, they called their people to them and scouts and hunters went out through the land to recover the loss. Through highways and byways, they searched, in all the hidden and out-of-the-way places they could find, but no one discovered the hiding-place of the crystal box.

Over time, changes began to happen in the land. The king and queen were still able monarchs, but want and sickness began to creep into the kingdom. The need to supply food and physical well-being occupied the people in a new way; desire for 'more and new' was replaced by the necessity to 'make do and mend'. Time passed and things worsened. Rewards and incentives for returning the box were regularly renewed, and each new season young hunters went out on the quest. None the less, only the stories of how it had once been remained in the land...

Well into the reign of the second king and queen, a young hunter returned to the court with some unexpected news. In an overgrown and unexplored domed cave at the edge of the land he had found one or two bags of gold and a handful of crystal fragments. With excitement the monarch received the shards and sent the warrior back to the cave with a team of searchers. Suspecting what might have happened, they were instructed to sift the floor of the cave and return with every fragment of glass which could be seen.

Meanwhile, the king and queen summoned the artists and glaziers to explore what might be done to restore the crystal box, and perhaps the fortunes of the land. Ultimately the most that could be accomplished was to melt down the glass fragments and recast the crystal into a new shape.

This time a globe was blown, with all the features of the land etched on its surface. The mountains were marked, and the seas and the meadows. The rough places were drawn, and the smooth plains and the sand-filled edges. The globe was to be hung in the middle of the throne room and, though it was no longer possible for the people's needs to be met from within its framework, it might serve the whole land as a symbol of hope and a focus for their stories which might lead to prosperity.

A decree was sent out that people from all parts of the land were to collect and prepare to send to the throne room treasures and mementoes of how it had been for their families in the prosperous days of the crystal box. The objects would be stored in a central place and the stories which were collected with them would be told, and retold, throughout the generations.

At this point, place the Bag of Bags in the middle of the circle (if it is not already displayed), and continue the narrative.

This bag might be part of the collection of mementoes and treasures which were returned in accordance with that decree. As we unpack the contents, notice which bag attracts your attention.

Move to the centre of the circle and open the Bag of Bags. Following the pattern of the first exercise, carefully set out the inner bags, one at a time. Invite people to choose one of the bags and return with it, unopened, to their place. You might continue the story by saying:

Over time, the specific stories of each bag have been lost or changed. The task of this part of the exercise is to discover or imagine something about the people of the land in the story from the bag you hold in your hand.

The listeners join in
Invite individuals to fully explore the bags they've chosen, using all their senses.
- How does it look?
- What does it feel like?
- Is there a specific aroma?

And further:
- What clues does the fabric give you?
- How is it fastened?
- What might the objects inside be?

Now allow people to open the bag and look carefully at the objects inside.

Continue the exercise as before, inviting each one to draw out from their considerations what might have been at work for the person who sent the object. When there has been time for this story to take shape, focus the attention of the group on the process of shaping the story they have claimed. Remind them of the importance of the beginning, the middle, and the end. Ask them to work through these steps and then review or rehearse their story before sharing it.

The initial sharing of the stories may be done in pairs, by either offering a period of time to be divided between them or keeping a time limit for each one to share. Allow time for reflection on the story shared. If the group is large, it may be appropriate to divide the group into fours or sixes, offering an opportunity, for all who want it, to practise sharing the story with a larger group. Perhaps each small group may then select one or two to share their stories with the larger group.

The end of the story

The last part of this application is to invite the group to return to the larger circle and, one by one, to return their individual bag to the Bag of Bags. As each bag is returned, invite something of the story developed to be shared—perhaps the identity of the 'owner', or the reason one of the items was included. If the group is small, it might be appropriate to invite all those who wish to, to tell their story of the bag; otherwise leave time for 'designated tellers' to share part of their tale.

In order to begin this part of the exercise, the pattern of your invitational dialogue might be something like this:

When the time for the Gathering Festival arrived, all the bearers of the family story bags gathered in the throne room. There was a time of celebration throughout all the land. Even though not everyone could personally share their memories, each one was represented by a speaker. One by one, the designated speakers brought their bag of treasure to the central place and offered to the group the story or memory it contained.

Step back and allow individuals to return their bags. Some may speak from their places in the circle; some may prefer to speak from the centre. Be sure to let people know the appropriate time-frame for the sharing.

When all the bags have been returned and all the stories told, you might close with a dialogue something like this:

When all was gathered in, there was great rejoicing. The celebrations went on for days and days. The stories that had been shared were told and retold. All the treasures that were offered were stored and valued. The former prosperity, as far as I know, never fully returned to the land. None the less, from that moment on there was a renewed sense of hope and healing throughout the land. Even if the original beauty had been broken and lost, the stories of the treasure, that could be neither lost nor stolen, offered windows of hope for healing and happiness.

Some reflection

Take a break. Be sure that the Bag of Bags is carefully closed, removed from the centre of the circle, and placed in its own resting-place.

Set aside a time later for the group to reflect upon the exercise. This is usually fruitful, both for the participants and for the exercise leader. Some questions which might be useful for guiding a reflective discussion include:

- ❖ Did this exercise enable you to claim, shape and share a story?
- ❖ What changes could enable the process to be more helpful to you?
- ❖ Could this pattern of work be applicable to groups to which you contribute?
- ❖ What connections with biblical material does this story suggest?

Telling Bible stories with the Bag of Bags

We do not need to be afraid to make connections between stories from literary sources, or our own experience and imagination, and stories from the Bible. Our creative, self-revealing God is present for us in all we think and say and do. As we focus on God in the scriptures, in prayer and study and worship, our insight and understanding are deepened. As we go out into the everyday world of family life, work and play, we come to recognize more clearly *God with us* in the ordinary. As we return to our common worship, bringing back to God our achievements and shortcomings, our joys and sadness, the process of healing and transformation continues and our faith grows.

We may trust our own deepening insight, and that of our children, to recognize the workings of God in our midst. Study, prayer and sharing help the process. Reflection on the resonance we explore suggests those avenues which are reliable and strong, and those which are less so.

Perhaps some connections with biblical material have already occurred to you as you have worked through the stories suggested by the Bag of Bags. Stories around the theme of 'treasure' seem particularly resonant—treasure lost or stolen, treasure hidden or found, treasure earthly or spiritual, treasure acquired at great cost and worth much effort and sacrifice. Listed below are some of the Bible stories which suggest themselves to me; your own list might include other selections. Any of them might appropriately follow on from this work or even be integrated into a retelling.

One of the individual bags might contain some coins or grain and a 'silver' cup: this could lead into a retelling by one of Joseph's brothers (Joseph and the silver cup: Genesis 44). Another might contain some fragments of stone, some jewellery, and a 'party hat'; it could prompt a story by Moses about God's forgiveness and the need for a second set of tablets (Moses and the tablets: Deuteronomy 5—6; 10). Another bag might contain a rolled up 'parchment' and lead into a telling about what happened when Josiah found the lost book of the Law (Josiah and the book of the Law: 2 Kings 22).

Other selections which might also lend themselves to work with the Bag of Bags include:

❖ The parables of the Kingdom (Matthew 13)
❖ The gifts of the Spirit (1 Corinthians 12)
❖ Tobias sets out with the angel (Tobit, from the Apocrypha)

Our God, the God of our fathers and mothers, is revealed in our history and is made known among us in our living and loving. The secular can inform the sacred and the sacred become known in the secular.

∞

CHAPTER FIVE

An inner landscape

Quiet your faces; be crossed every thumb;
Fix on me deep your eyes;
And out of my mind a story shall come,
Old, and lovely, and wise.

WALTER DE LA MARE

There are a variety of approaches to preparing a story for telling. We have discussed in previous exercises the *three-line skeleton*, *cartoon outline*, and *stepping into the story*. Each of these approaches can be equally well applied to retelling personal experience as to biblical material. When working with lived experience, we have memory to draw upon as a resource for supplying the details of setting and the 'feel' of the characters involved. When working with biblical material, we approach those aspects of the story from a position at least once removed.

This exercise offers a response. It is designed to encourage the awareness of a possible inner landscape from which to retell the stories of Jesus. It incorporates a technique for personal reflection that may be adapted and extended more widely. This exercise will focus on:

- ❖ enabling the inner landscape
- ❖ processing the visualization for retelling
- ❖ further reflection—timing, feedback, reshaping
- ❖ a possible retelling from an 'eye-witness' point of view

Enabling the inner landscape

Select the material

Choose the Bible passage(s) with which you will work. It may be a reading set for a particular time in the church's year or a selection of texts focused on a particular event in the life and ministry of Jesus. For the purposes of this exercise, I am working with the theme of Jesus calling the disciples. The main reading assigned for the day of the event is Mark 1:14–20. (Additional references appear in Mark 2:13–17, as well as in Matthew 4:18–22; 9:9–13; 10:2–4; Luke 5:1–11, 27–31; 6:13–16 and John 1:35–51.)

Jesus came to Galilee, proclaiming the good news of God and saying, 'The time is fulfilled, and the kingdom of God has come near; repent, and believe in the good news.'

As Jesus passed along the Sea of Galilee, he saw Simon and his brother Andrew casting a net into the sea—for they were fishermen. And Jesus said to them, 'Follow me and I will make you fish for people.' And immediately they left their nets and followed him. As he went a little farther, he saw James son of Zebedee and his brother John, who were in their boat mending the nets. Immediately he called them; and they left their father Zebedee in the boat with the hired men, and followed him (Mark 1:14–20).

Jesus went out again beside the sea; the whole crowd gathered around him, and he taught them. As he was walking along, he saw Levi (also called Matthew) son of Alphaeus sitting at the tax booth, and he said to him, 'Follow me.' And he got up and followed him (Mark 2:13–15).

Jesus found Philip and said to him, 'Follow me.' … Philip found Nathanael and said to him, 'We have found him about whom Moses in the law and also the prophets wrote… Come and see' (John 1:43, 45–46).

Read the passages thoroughly

Read with the particular intent to retain an overview of the whole event. Be aware of how it begins, what action develops through the story, and how it ends. Notice the location of the event(s). What details does the text offer about the setting? What do you know about such a place from your own experience?

Be aware of the main characters mentioned in the text. What aspects of their personality or character are mentioned? Do you remember additional information about them from other biblical material? What particularly stands out for you regarding personal appearance or behaviour in the story?

Close the book and find a quiet place

Once you are familiar with the text, put it aside. The aim of this exercise is to know the life of Jesus better and to have a clearer inner landscape from which to tell his story. With this desire in mind, choose a place where you can be quiet and undisturbed for twenty minutes to half an hour.

Focus on the purpose of the reflection

For the example, the purpose of this exercise will be to become more aware of what it might have been like to have been called by Jesus and to have gone with him.

Settle yourself

Seat yourself comfortably in an upright position—back straight, feet on the floor, hands comfortably on your lap. Release the tension in your shoulders and neck; draw and exhale a couple of deep breaths. Set aside, as much as possible, your thoughts and feelings about the other events and tasks of the day. Give yourself permission for your mind and heart and imagination to work faithfully together on this story of Jesus. Now close your eyes, or at least lower your eyelids, to give prominence to your inner spaces.

Allow the setting of the story to form

In the freest inner space available to you, allow the scene from the passage you have prepared to take form in your reflective space. Let the landscape take shape. Notice the trees and plants and bushes, the places of water and of dry land. This story of Jesus begins by the Sea of Galilee. Be aware of the additional details in the scene—the shore line, the boats. What else is in the scene... buildings or storage places, pieces of equipment, other objects? Notice the colours and shapes in the water and the sky.

Place the characters

Which of the characters in the story will be in the scene at the beginning? Notice where they are placed and what they might be doing when the action starts. At the lakeside when Jesus arrives, Simon and Andrew will be fishing with nets.

Might there be other people in the scene, not mentioned specifically, carrying out ordinary activities? Are there small groups of people or even the beginning of a crowd? Could there be children playing or animals or other creatures present at the start of the action?

Decide where you will be in the scene. Will you be one of the characters? Will you be watching from a neutral place? Will you be alone or interacting with others?

Notice the mood and the atmosphere. What is the weather like? What might be going on between people in the background when the action starts?

Let Jesus enter the scene and start the action

When everything is in place, Jesus enters the scene and the action begins. Give yourself permission to allow the story to unfold and to watch what happens as you go along. Be aware of sights and sounds and changing moods. Are there colours, odours or aromas? As you watch the story unfolding, notice your own thoughts and feelings as well as the interactions of those around you.

Take the time necessary for the event to come to closure

Allow the events in your own interior landscape to unfold until the interaction ends. How does closure come? Does the scene fade in your visualization? Do Jesus and the principal characters move out of sight? Since this represents only a portion of a larger scenario, our stopping-places represent more of a pause than a permanent ending.

Allow the visualization to come to an end

When a clear pause or stopping-place is reached, give yourself time to pause and bring the visualization to a close. Perhaps, if you are one of the characters, there are things you might want to say. Even as a neutral observer, you might think it appropriate to speak to or interact with someone in the scene before taking your leave. When all that is necessary has been completed, slowly refocus on your quiet sitting-place. Draw and exhale one or two breaths. Open your eyes. Move your head, neck, shoulders and arms. Stretch out your legs and back.

Take time to capture the experience

Before moving on to the next task, give yourself about ten or fifteen minutes to record the experience. Perhaps you would like to make one or two notes about what happened, or even a series of sketches. Recall your own thoughts or feelings as the story unfolded. Did anything happen that you did not expect? Is there any intervention you would like to have made or anyone to whom you would like to have spoken? As the purpose of this is to enable a 'memory' from which to retell the story, you will be visiting the material again; even so, it might be helpful later to have a note of these initial reactions.

Processing the visualization for retelling

The challenge of this exercise now is to tell what you 'saw', or felt, or experienced, in a shape which will be informative and attractive to the people who are the listeners and which will fit into the appropriate event and timeframe.

Recall the visualization

At one level, working with a visualization is very much like working with a memory. The important thing is to catch the experience as a whole. Go back over your visualization and be sure you remember the entire story. You might like to use the pattern of the three-line skeleton, or even the cartoon outline, to help you. How did it start? How did it end? What were one or two significant turning points along the way? Recall one or two of the background details that caught your attention. Make a note of any character or incident that particularly caught your attention.

You might like to write down what you experienced, as if you were writing a letter, or sending an e-mail, to a friend. Some people find this a helpful step in the creative process.

Identify the listeners and the event

It is important to be aware of the age of the listeners, the size of the group, and the interests of those for whom the story is to be told. While the substance of the story of Jesus calling the disciples is the same and equally important across the age range, the particular language and the length you choose for the telling will vary according to the hearer's profile. Is this for an adult study session, a children's group, or a family event?

The reason for the telling also is significant. Do the listeners expect some teaching, a bit of entertainment, or an inspirational message? Your presentation needs to vary according to the formality of the occasion, the size of the group, the reason for which every-one has come together. It might be equally relevant to include a telling of this story in a regular morning worship service, a mid-week children's club, or even as one item in a longer programme of storytelling. None the less, the length and language and introduction to the same story would likely be quite different in each situation.

Define a context for the story

While it is not inappropriate to use a retelling of biblical narrative material in story form, it is important that the listener is as integral to the experience as the teller and the story itself. It is important that the listeners know what to expect and that they are actually involved in a shared experience as the story is told. In presenting the story to a Sunday morning children's group, the story of Jesus and his friends becomes the focus for the day's prayer, sharing and creative work. The children and the leader would probably be sitting together on a rug or in a circle, focused and ready to listen and respond to the story being told.

This Gospel narrative retold in story form might equally be appropriate as part of the Ministry of the Word in a regular service of worship. Once, when the Marcan passage was the Gospel reading set for the day, I used a retelling as part of the sermon in a Sunday service. The first part of the address contained all the 'teaching and preaching'—I introduced the theme, explained what I was going to do, and made the points it seemed appropriate to bring out.

Next I invited the congregation to 'try something different'... to reserve all their current thoughts and feelings and to allow themselves to hear this story of the beginning of Jesus' ministry as new. I invited them to 'switch on' their imaginations or inner video recorders and perhaps even to 'watch' the story as it unfolds. I think my opening sentence was something like, 'We enter the story in Mark by the Sea of Galilee. Jesus is there... walking along the shore.' Perhaps from your own experience you can think of a stronger, better beginning!

Enjoy the experience yourself

One of the aspects of storytelling not often discussed is the legitimate pleasure the teller may take in the process. We have a high expectation that the listeners will enjoy the experience; in fact, much of our preparatory work is structured with that goal in mind. Since we've had a critical choice in the selection of the material, we usually believe that the story itself is a good one and worth the telling. We may also give ourselves permission to enjoy the experience.

Perhaps, for some, the pleasure comes from the satisfaction of completing a challenge; for others it might be associated with a good feeling that comes from making something personally valuable available to others. Often a deep feeling of contentment comes through an awareness of a special energy—something like a relationship—shared among the listeners, the teller and the characters of the story. Not the least of the pleasant aspects of this art and craft is the delight in the actual physical communication of the material—the sound and feeling of forming the words, moving the body, following the movement of the story with gesture and stance.

Too often we allow ourselves to be aware only of our more uncomfortable feelings. We experience the pressure and uncertainty in the preparation stages while trying to shape the story so it will be 'just right'. We can talk about the feelings of anxiety before a presentation, even while acknowledging the helpful role these feelings have in releasing energy for what is to be accomplished. Many have a hard time letting go of feelings of disappointment which come from not quite reaching individual targets of attainment.

All these feelings are real and recognizable. We may also give equal place and open space to our feelings of pleasure and enjoyment. Sometimes the moment at the end of a presentation is a time for sharing of pleasure; sometimes there are words spoken in private after the event which may be encouraging and heart-warming. To my thinking, the most lasting and perhaps most integral pleasure of the experience of story-sharing comes from within the process of the telling itself. We may own this, be aware of personal pleasure in the preparation stages, and allow ourselves to enjoy the telling itself. As part of the teller's own experience, this sense of delight becomes shared out and passed around among the listeners as well.

An example of a possible retelling

Retelling a story from a personal point of view offers a different connection between the listener and the teller. When retelling a lived experience, we speak with confidence about what we saw, the things we heard, how we felt at the time. We share this with our listeners in such a fashion that they may understand what happened —that, in a way, they may actually be there, too. The energy and involvement communicated through the telling also seems to invite the listener into the experience.

Retelling a story based on a visualization can offer a similar opportunity. From the position you occupied in the exercise, how would you begin the story of Jesus calling the disciples? What link could you establish with the event? This is one possible beginning. Notice how the emphasis and intimacy change when spoken from a first-person point of view. Notice also what can be included and what might be left out in this different application.

It was midday. There was a bit of a wind and quite a few people were moving around beside the lake. I probably wouldn't have paid much attention to what was going on, but when Simon laid down his net and walked away I knew something unusual was happening. Simon never walked away without a catch. You could really depend on the fact that he'd stand there all day if necessary in order to bring in the fish. You could really rely on Simon. If he set out to do something, he did it.

I also noticed that his brother Andrew didn't give Simon a hard time when he put down the net. Andrew even stopped his work and went with him. That was different, too. It really looked quite strange to see them both walk away. The third member of their party was Jesus. I'd seen him around before. He was more or less local. Somehow he was related to John, the wild man who lived in the desert. Once when a group of women and men were moved by what John was saying and were being baptized by him, Jesus showed up. People said John was rather embarrassed but he baptized Jesus, just like the others.

I thought there must be some kind of emergency or something, but the three men didn't go far, or do much. They just stood there on the shore, talking. Well, at least, Jesus was talking. I wasn't really close enough to hear what they were saying; only snatches of their words drifted my way. Something about 'repent' and 'good news'.

I guess that's why I thought of the Baptist. When Jesus said, 'Come with me' and moved off, I followed along, too.

Good thing they weren't paying any attention to me. I wasn't going to stay long but I was curious. As the three men walked along, I followed on. I became even more curious when Jesus and the others got to Zebedee's boat. He and his sons were sitting in their boat, pulled high up on the shore, and mending their nets. They seemed to have something to say to everyone who passed by.

When Jesus went up to have a word, both James and John climbed out over the side and walked away with him and Simon and Andrew. They left the old man in the boat with only the hired help to finish the job! I really thought they'd take a piece of their father's mind with them, so it was very surprising that no one got upset. The whole scene looked as if everything that was happening was quite ordinary. Extraordinary, really.

This is one possible retelling from the passage in Mark. If you were to carry on with this dialogue, what would you say next? How would you bring this part of the story to closure? Has enough already been said? Remember that the last line is very important for a story well told.

Further reflection: awareness, feedback and flexibility, reshaping

Once the story has been shared and the event brought to an end, there is one more step to consider. It is important to give time to personal and shared observations and to practise some critical reflection on your own telling.

Awareness

There may be a variety of good ways to do this. One 'way in' to some personal reflection is to notice your own comfort level. Here are some questions:

❖ Did you have a good time?
❖ What was one high spot?

❖ Did you feel uncomfortable?
❖ Can you identify the cause?

Resonance or harmony between me (as teller) and the listener is one of my own indicators of when things are going well. This harmony gives me a sense of well-being and pleasure. A particular high spot in one telling of a story may give me courage to repeat that aspect of the presentation on another occasion. I have noticed, however, that each group is unique. While one strong aspect of a story may be reliably well received, the listening group's response will be really quite different with each retelling.

Feedback and flexibility

Feelings of discomfort are also useful indicators. Awareness of discomfort is not something to be avoided but an understanding that can be used to good advantage. It can indicate missed communication between the teller and the listener, when the listener's response is different from what was expected. The teller can respond by changing the length or language as the story continues. Sometimes a sense of harmony can be restored. My experience suggests that at other times the best thing to do is to bring the story to a speedy end and move on to another piece of 'tried and tested' material.

During one of my first storytelling events in a local school, I began to tell a folk tale which had been very popular when I was growing up in the United States. I had told this story to my classes when I was a teacher in Washington, DC, and expected a similar response from the same-aged children near my home in London. It was surprising to me to receive very little feedback as I developed what promised to be a very funny set of circumstances.

When I continued to receive very blank looks, and not even the teachers were offering me polite laughter, I brought the story to a speedy end and hurried on to another piece of material I'd already told to a UK group with some success. Later in the staff room, I had a chance to ask the classroom teacher why nobody seemed to like my folk tale. 'Well,' she said, 'you kept talking about a squash which grew bigger and bigger and escaped from the field. All I could see was a big plastic bottle of orange liquid running down the road. It just didn't make sense.' Even when I retold the story as 'The Quick Running Marrow' it was never quite the same as before.

Sometimes, as in this case, it is possible to come to an understanding of the dynamics of a situation; sometimes it isn't. Through working repeatedly with a given story, I've discovered quite a few words which have meant one thing to me, the teller, and something very different to the listeners—and the cause has not always been due to my ethnic origin! Usage of words varies from one area of the country to another. In some cases, common words have been purposely redefined to create a local jargon or bit of 'in talk'. Local dialects can endow very familiar words with unfamiliar applications. Experience helps the teller to notice and adapt in such situations.

I have also discovered that certain words and characters in stories turn out to have associations with cultural and religious beliefs which cause a particular group of people to respond in an unexpected way. One group of children were very uncomfortable with a folk tale about a Hoop Snake. Another group of children were not willing to put on the 'little pig' masks which I'd brought to help tell another story. I present both of those stories differently now.

Sometimes the dynamic which causes a distance between the teller and the listener is caused by unequal expectations, the time of day, or a situation operating outside the event, of which the teller may not ever become aware. While a brief conversation with the organizer of an event can help the storyteller to be prepared for local preferences and idiosyncrasies, the unexpected is usually a feature of the experience—for the teller as well as the listener! Flexibility comes with experience and a willingness to adjust to the needs of the moment.

Reshaping

The fruit of the reflection on the storytelling is a stronger, more clearly formed tale to tell. It isn't true that the reworking of familiar material becomes boring and tedious. In fact, the more opportunity one has to clarify and focus a particular selection, the more interesting and vigorous it becomes. Such items, carefully reworked and sympathetically redefined, become foundational aspects of a mature repertoire. Those very stories which have survived sometimes uncomfortable passages become the reliable resources that tellers turn to in future times of unexpected need. To be able to turn to a well-formed and reliably invitational narrative frees a teller to continue to experiment with new material.

It is also true that working with narratives from our religious traditions offers levels of insight and aspects of interpretation which cannot be exhausted. Such material offers to both the teller and the listener scope for possible connections that are way beyond the awareness of even the most experienced. This understanding helps to keep the teller faithfully committed to retelling the truth of the tale as it was received. The adjustments to language, the length, and sensitive reshaping which each individual brings to the retelling, come to fruition in the extent to which each listener also enters the story, and names and claims their own personal and corporate experience. A story well told becomes a seed well sown.

∞

CHAPTER SIX

Story cloths: Preparation and use for biblical storytelling

Story cloths... provided a way to recall the history and hope that bound a group of people to a common purpose.

ANN WINN, IN *THE BANNER BOX: A NATIONAL CURRICULUM RESOURCE*, HEREFORDSHIRE COUNCIL CULTURAL SERVICES, 1999. [1]

The concept of the story cloth is an old one. Traditionally, the shapes and figures on such cloths provided visual clues to the stories and sacred traditions important to a group of people. Historically, they have appeared as hangings, tent decorations, even bedcovers. Itinerant storytellers, especially those in India, made good use of story cloths to draw people to themselves and to provide a lead into telling stories. Even today, returning travellers report being drawn to such tellers and, on occasion, have even understood themselves to have been worked into the tale.

I saw story cloths for the first time in the college studio of artist Pauline Vincent. Following on from various works collected there, we conceived the idea of a pair of story cloths which could provide a focus for the telling and retelling of stories from the Bible. One panel was designed to focus on shapes and symbols connected with the Hebrew scriptures. The second cloth was planned to offer visual connections with the life and ministry of Jesus and the developing Christian communities.

The sections in this chapter include:
* a plan for the creation of the story cloths
* one approach to telling stories with the cloths
* some reflection on the process

The creation of the cloths

The application of telling the stories of our Christian tradition from story cloths seemed interesting. In her book *The Inner Story: Myth and Symbol in the Bible and Literature*, Helen Luke makes a strong case for working with such visual material.

We can say, 'I believe in this or that,' and assert the truth of many doctrines, but these things will not affect the soul of any one of us unless in some way we experience their meaning through intense response to the images conveyed in story.[2]

Our aim was to present a simple and accessible pattern which might be made available for small group work and community development in schools and churches, for work with adults as well as children, and appropriate for all-age events.

A beginning

To begin with, we prepared two pieces of plain calico trimmed and hemmed to a size of approximately 118 cm (46.5 in) x 136 cm (54 in). These provided the fabric 'canvas' and included a finished rod-pocket at the top of about 4 cm (1.5 in) to enable the cloth to be more easily hung. (Two cotton bed sheets, appropriately trimmed, might be equally useful.) We intended to use a paste-resist method and cold water dye for the creation of the shapes on the cloth. Such techniques would be safe and accessible for groups with a wide range of ages and abilities.

The first cloth

Using a paste mixture of flour and water and stiff bristled brushes, we began the creation. A sectioned column grew at the centre of the first cloth: it suggested a palm-type tree sprouting from some small seeds placed toward the bottom. Was it the tree of the knowledge of good and evil from Eden, or a sheltering palm in a desert oasis, or the family tree which connected all the twelve tribes of the children of Israel? Shapes and patterns were traced in the sections of the body of the tree—a male and female shape; a slithery serpent; steps and handles, which made one large section toward the top of the tree resemble a ladder. Were those angels that seemed to be going up and down on either side?

Several branches spread out from the central column to the left and right, dividing the surface into roughly six sections. We hoped to suggest figures and shapes from which the many stories from the Hebrew scriptures could be told. We discussed the stories we felt it was important to make accessible and agreed upon most of the shapes to include. Some of the shapes simply presented themselves as we went along.

The sun appeared in one corner of the cloth and the stars and moon in two others. The moon was shown in different phases and with different groups of stars: it was one way of suggesting a change of seasons and the movement between darkness and light. There was a large tent-like shape in one corner and what might be a walled city a bit further along the bottom; both included figures of people who seemed to be going in and out.

We drew a covered boat in one of the six sections, and also a whale-like shape with an active human figure inside. There were some fish and a woman tending a baby in a rounded basket. There was water flowing out of a rock and definitely some dry ground near what might be a high wall of water.

In one of the six sections, figures were blowing instruments and banging cymbals, and one was playing a harp. In another section, one figure held up two large tablet shapes, and there were pyramids and a kneeling figure and a bush which seemed to be on fire. With wax, we formed some fearsome creatures in another section; a warrior with a strange shaped sword; and three small figures who also seemed to be surrounded by fire. Male and female shapes were visible in postures of celebration and supplication; some were seen to be gathering food or tending animals; others were simply asleep.

A broad circle around the outside of all this seemed to hold the sections together, and we traced more shapes of fish and birds and animals which seemed able to move across the borders. One bird held a branch in its beak and another group of winged creatures might have been a flight of angels.

The second cloth

The patterns and organization of the second cloth reflected the pattern of the first. A branching 'tree' provided the central column and focus for the cloth; it had a strong cruciform shape and in one part even suggested the trunk of a really strong vine with sprouting branches. A circle of paste contained the figures as before, and the shapes of seeds and leaves and fruit seemed to blossom and ripen across the boundaries and off the edge of the cloth.

The space was once again divided into six sections. The human shapes, symbols, and other forms which were patterned within them were meant to refer to the life and ministry of Jesus and of the developing Christian communities. Angels figured in the sections; they were speaking to women and men and in one case attending what might have been a tomb. There was definitely a family grouping with a swaddled infant in one section and several groups of individuals throughout the sections.

People were standing up and lying down; one was being carried on a bed and several were in or near water. There was a very seaworthy-looking boat in one section, with a 'fishy' sail and a strong-looking figure in the bow. In other places, water was being drawn and seeds were being sown and one figure could be seen clinging to and peering out of the upper branches of the tree. At the open top of the central 'tree', an open-mouthed face had visible 'breath' and nearby was a clear cross, etched with a lamb at the centre and surrounded by four splendid figures—one of which was a lion, another an eagle.

The roots of this second tree were very clearly an outgrowth of the fruits of the former. The style of the figures, their shapes and clothing definitely linked the two cloths. The same dyes were selected to finish both cloths as an additional way of clearly indicating that they were a pair.

Finishing the cloths

We chose red and blue cold water dyes to colour the cloths. The dye was thickened with a dye thickener until it had the consistency of jam. First we painted on the red dye around the figures on each cloth. When the red dye was dry, the next step was to cover it with paste and leave it to dry. The main body of the cloths were then dyed blue; once again by applying the thickened dye with a brush. Variation in the colour that was created by the overlapping red, white and blue areas provided depth of colour to the cloths and interest to the scenes. (See fuller references in *The Banner Box*, Herefordshire Council Cultural Services, 1999.)

When the colour was thoroughly dry, we removed all the layers of paste by dampening the cloths and scraping away as much of the paste as possible. What remained of the paste was removed by gently rinsing the cloths in cold water. A final pressing with a hot iron finished the cloths and they were hung and ready for use.

Old Testament

These images suggest stories of the children of God. Can you see Jonah in the belly of the whale? Can you find Moses and the tablets of stone? What images might you have included?

New Testament

These figures suggest stories from the life of Jesus. There are fish and goats and human figures in both cloths. How might you have arranged the images? What additional figures would also be appropriate?

How to tell stories with the cloths

Continuing work with the story cloths has effectively invited individual creativity as well as promoting group development. These cloths, and those which have been developed from them, have been seen to offer a stimulating focus for sharing Bible stories. When hanging side by side, the story cloths provide a visual focus and multiple points of departure for storytelling sessions. The cloths I've described were made with an adult audience or all-age events in mind; such a pattern might equally well be followed using the bold, simple shapes most appropriate for the younger child.

In the exercise which follows, the approach is one that is appropriate for work with older children or a group of mixed ages; the pattern can be equally effective when adapted for different age groups. The two stories I will use are:

❖ the story of the prophet Jonah (Jonah 1—4)

❖ Jesus calming the storm (Matthew 8:23–27; Mark 4:35–41; Luke 8:22–25)

Getting started

The first task in a storytelling session might be to introduce the concept of the cloths themselves and to invite a process of familiarization with the pictures they present. The dialogue for such a presentation might begin like this:

These two cloths present people and events drawn from across the whole contents of what is written in the Bible. One cloth concentrates on the lives and history of the Hebrew people (point to the first cloth). The other traces the life and ministry of Jesus and those who followed him (indicate the second cloth).

Take a good look at both cloths. Here are some questions to help us reflect.

❖ What do you notice about the cloths? (Allow time for responses from the group. Accept the observations which are offered, repeating when necessary in order for everyone to hear what is said.)

- How do you think they were made? (Be willing to supply the information that the figures were painted on with flour and water paste and then the dye was added.)
- How are the cloths alike? What are some of the differences between them?

Now let's concentrate on the figures on the cloths.
- What figures do you see? What are they doing? Each figure or group of figures might be related to one of the stories in the Bible.
- What stories do you recognize on this cloth?

(Indicate the second cloth.)

Remember that the stories on this cloth refer to Jesus and his friends.
- What stories do you think of when you look at these figures?
- This looks like an angel. Perhaps the angel is speaking to this woman. What do you think the story might be about?
- What other stories of Jesus do you think of when you look at these figures?

(Indicate the first cloth.)

Remember that the stories on this cloth are about things that happened before Jesus was born. The figures of animals and people suggest the stories of the Hebrew people. They believed that God was with them from the earliest times. This looks like a very large boat with some animals on the deck.
- What do you think that story might be about?
- Are there figures that suggest other stories that you know from this part of the Bible?

If you are working within a limited timeframe, this could be enough to accomplish in one session. Retelling a story drawn from a figure from each of the cloths could be spread over one or two subsequent sessions. If, however, you are using this as an introductory exercise in a longer session, you might proceed at this point to focus on one figure or scene and lead into the story you wish to tell. For example (still working with the Hebrew scriptures cloth):

This shape looks very much like a large fish with a human figure inside. Do you know who this story might be about? The man inside the fish's belly might be Jonah. Jonah was a person for whom God had a mission.

The story of Jonah

The preparation
Your personal preparation for the telling of this story would naturally have been done before this presentation. Such preparation would include a thorough reading of the text in order to be familiar with the story as a whole. It might also include some additional background reading or survey of biblical commentaries.

The use of the cartoon outline described in Chapter Two, 'Shaping the story', would be appropriate for preparing the story of Jonah. This exercise could help you to remember the order in which the events in Jonah's experience took place. The first four frames might include 'cartoons' to identify:
1 God's call and Jonah's turning away.
2 The angry sea and the worried sailors praying.
3 The sailors talking to Jonah and tossing him overboard.
4 Jonah in the belly of the fish.

The second four frames could recall:
5 Jonah in Nineveh.
6 The king and the people's repentance.
7 Jonah resting under a leafy plant.
8 Jonah standing beside a withered plant.

The amount of detail and the language of the retelling would need to reflect the nature of the listeners and the timing of the event. One retelling of the story might be as follows.

The retelling

1. Jonah was a man of faith who loved God and had vowed to serve God. One day the word of God came to Jonah and asked him to go to a great city. He was to tell the people of Nineveh about God and to call them to change their ways and live a good life. He was to warn them that if they did not change, great destruction would come to their land.

Jonah knew that God forgave people who were sorry for wrong-doing and who tried to put things right. But Jonah didn't do what God asked. Instead, he went in another direction. Jonah went to the seaside town of Joppa. There he found a ship which was going on a journey to Tarshish and he paid his fare to travel with them.

2. They hadn't been long at sea when God sent a great wind and storm and the ship began to be strongly tossed about. There were people from many lands and faiths on board and they all prayed to their gods to save the ship. When the captain did not see Jonah, he went to look for him. Finding Jonah asleep below deck, the captain cried, 'What are you doing asleep? Get up and pray to your god and maybe the storm will stop.' But the storm only grew worse.

3. Finally, in desperation, the sailors cast lots to see who might be to blame for what was happening to them. When the lot fell to Jonah, he told them that he was a Hebrew. He told them that he worshipped the Lord, the God who created heaven, the sea and the dry land. He also told them that he was running away from God, and that God was probably angry. Jonah said that if they threw him overboard, the ship would most likely be saved.

The sailors didn't want to be so cruel. They tried throwing away the cargo and even rowing toward land, but nothing seemed to work. The storm grew worse and worse. Finally they did as Jonah asked and threw him overboard. The people on board prayed that God would save Jonah and not blame them for killing him.

4.   When Jonah fell into the water, a very big fish came by and swallowed him up. The story as told in the Bible says that God, who created everything at the beginning of time, sent this fish to save Jonah. Jonah was in the belly of the fish for three days. Some of the details suggested in Hebrew *midrash* say that God saved Jonah and the fish together and that at first it was comfortable for Jonah. Others suggest that Jonah could see out through the fish's eyes and that the fish swam around showing him all the delights of the sea.[3]

Finally, however, it happened, Jonah decided that he wanted to do what God wanted him to. He was thankful that God had saved him and he prayed to God, saying, '…out of the belly of Sheol you have heard my voice… What I have vowed, I will pay. Deliverance belongs to the Lord.' And in that moment, God spoke to the fish and the fish spewed Jonah out upon dry land.

5.   Once again the word of God came to Jonah. 'Get up, go to Nineveh, that great city, and proclaim the message I tell you.' This time Jonah went to Nineveh. It was a very big city; it took three days to walk across. When he had been walking for one day, Jonah cried, 'Forty days more and Nineveh will be overthrown!'

6.   The people heard Jonah and they believed what he said. They were sorry for the things they were doing wrong and they wanted to live a good life. The Bible says that everyone, great and small, put on sackcloth and proclaimed a fast. Even the king was sorry. When he heard what Jonah had said, he sent out a message to the whole area: 'All people must turn from their evil ways and stop the violence that is in their hands. Who knows? God may relent. God may forgive us so that we do not perish.'

7.   When God saw that the people were truly sorry, that they were making changes in the way they were treating each other, God did relent and did not bring great destruction upon them. This made Jonah very cross. He spoke to God about his feelings. 'This is what

I said would happen when I was running away from you. I knew that you are a gracious God, slow to anger and abounding in steadfast love, and ready to relent from punishing. I knew you wouldn't hurt the people of Nineveh if they were truly sorry. But you have made me look silly. I said they would be destroyed and now nothing has happened.'

God answered Jonah with a question. 'Is it right for you to be angry?' But Jonah was angry. He went out of the city and climbed a hill nearby. He built a shelter for himself and sat under it in the shade to see what would happen to the city. He was very uncomfortable.

Then God reached out to Jonah. God caused a bush to come up over him, to cover him and give him some comfort. Jonah was very happy about the bush.

8. When dawn came the next morning, a worm came and ate all the leaves off the bush so that the bush withered. When the sun rose, it beat down on Jonah's head and he was angry again... angry this time that the bush had wasted away.

Then God reached out to Jonah once more. 'Is it right for you to be angry about the bush?' asked God.

'Yes,' said Jonah, 'very angry indeed.'

'You are concerned about the bush,' answered God. 'A bush with whose planting and growing you had nothing to do. It came into being in a night and perished in a night. Should I not be concerned about that great city Nineveh? There are more than a hundred and twenty thousand persons there who do not know their right hand from their left... their right from their wrong... and also many animals.'

The Hebrew *midrash* says that then Jonah realized the lesson God was showing him in the bush. He understood that it was more important for the people to repent and to live a good life than that he should have a good reputation. Then Jonah was sorry for being angry. He bowed down to God and prayed, 'O God, may the world be guided by Thy goodness.'[4]

A story about Jesus in the boat

The preparation[5]

One of the interesting ways to use the two cloths is to work with the stories surrounding similar themes and subjects from the two parts of the Bible. The story of Jonah might lead in to several stories about Jesus. The story of the mission of the prophet Jonah to the people of Nineveh surely demonstrates God's concern beyond the wider borders of Israel. Some see in Jonah a prefiguring of the coming Messiah, a prototype of Jesus. In his teaching, Jesus makes reference to the 'sign of the prophet Jonah'. He goes on to draw a parallel between the three days and nights Jonah spent in the belly of the great fish and the three days the 'Son of Man' will spend in the 'heart of the earth'.

For this pair of story sessions, we might notice the relationship of both Jonah and Jesus with the elements. Jonah was at the mercy of the wind and sea; when he was in the boat, his prayer could not stem the force of the elements. In fact, the story suggests that the storm was generated by Jonah's behaviour being out of harmony with God's mission for him. Jesus, on the other hand, had control of the winds and the sea. When he was in the boat and awakened from sleep, his words calmed the storm. Jesus' watchful presence with his friends was surely where God wanted him to be.

The shape of the boat on the second cloth, and the presence of a strong peaceful figure in the bow, gives a positive impetus to a retelling of Jesus in the boat with his friends. The first step in the preparation is to read through the biblical accounts. In these instances the scenes appear in more than one of the Gospels. Notice the resonance and differences. Perhaps it is appropriate to follow one reference for further work. I've chosen to follow primarily the account in Mark.

The use of a meditative visualization approach to further preparation could be helpful for this passage. (See Chapter Five, 'An inner landscape', for full development of the approach.) Remember the steps involved:

❖ **Focus on the purpose of the reflection.** In this case it will be to be aware of what it might have been like to be with Jesus in the boat.

❖ **Settle yourself into a quiet place.** Still the body, thoughts, and feelings to open a reflective space for yourself.

❖ **Allow the setting to form in this inner space.** Notice the land, the sky, the sea. How does the landscape look? Are the colours bright or dull? Add the boats and other objects. Now place the people and other figures in the scene. What place do you occupy in this scenario?

❖ **Let Jesus enter the scene and start the action.** Watch what develops. What sounds do you hear? Are you aware of any odours or aromas? As you watch the story unfolding, notice your own thoughts and feelings.

❖ **Allow the visualization to come to an end.** Slowly come out of the visualization space.

❖ **Reflect on the process you've just experienced.** How did it start? What was the ending? Was there a main turning point, or perhaps two along the way? Perhaps you will want to make some notes of particular things you noticed, smelled, felt, or thought for use in later retellings.

Now try retelling what you've just been working with. Choose a beginning sentence and a good, strong closing line. Be clear about the midpoint of the story you will tell. Since the story grows out of a figure on the story cloth, it is good to begin by focusing the listener's attention back on to the cloth.

Practise telling the story out aloud. Perhaps you are happy to speak to an imaginary audience in your own room or into a tape. Even better, try out your new story on a friend or family member; the helpful feedback from a present listener is very encouraging indeed. However you are able to arrange these experimental 'run throughs', don't forget to reflect afterwards on what you've said. Think about what went well, what you might leave out or what you might add in at another retelling.

A retelling

Having done the preparation just described, here is one possible way to retell the story.

Looking at the figures on this cloth reminds me of many of the stories about Jesus and his friends. Here are some friends standing in a group. Here is the figure of a man who has climbed a tree. Here are some friends sharing their bread. Here is a boat floating in the water. Look at the smiling figure in the prow. This reminds me of the story of one of the times Jesus and his friends went out together in a boat.

Jesus was living and teaching near the Lake of Galilee. People in the area came to hear him speak and to bring those who were sick to him for healing. Jesus told them about the loving God of all creation who cared for all people. He reminded people of the way to live so they might show love to God in return. His stories were about the way this kind of living could bring the kingdom of heaven into their daily lives.

Some people stayed with Jesus to help him and to learn more about what he was teaching. On one occasion, Jesus and his friends got into a boat to cross the lake to visit another town. His friends were sailing or rowing the boat and Jesus fell asleep on a cushion in the back of the boat. While they were crossing the lake, some very strong winds came whipping down from the hills. High waves formed on the lake and the boat was being roughly tossed about. Water was pouring in on them and even though some of the friends were fishermen on this lake, they became afraid that the boat would be filled with water or overturned.

Jesus was still asleep. The friends woke him up, saying, 'Teacher! We're in danger. The boat is likely to be swamped.' As Jesus woke up, he seemed to speak to the wind and he said to the rough water, 'Peace! Be still!' The Bible says that then the wind ceased and there was calm.

When Jesus spoke to his friends, he asked them a question. 'Why are you afraid? Have you still no faith?' Such an experience made his friends wonder even more who this man was who seemed to be able make the wind and water obey him.

Some reflection on the process

It is always important to consider how we might give ourselves credit for work well done as well as to make notes for the future about how the next attempt might be improved. Casual reflection while we're collecting materials or travelling home might be enough, if time is short and pressure high. Some record of the thoughts which occur will definitely be worth keeping for reference; a file of such records which grows over time will become an invaluable resource for personal and professional growth and development.

These questions might prompt your reflection:

❖ How did this exercise and the telling that followed it work for you?

❖ Was the listening group attracted by the figures on the cloths?

❖ How were the stories told received by the listeners?

❖ What other stories did the listeners identify from the cloth? Are any of these appropriate to use in a follow-up session?

❖ What other ideas for using the cloths occurred to you?

NOTES

1   In the same publication, see also various illustrations by Pauline Vincent in addition to a section on 'Scrap Materials'.

2   Luke, Helen M., *The Inner Story: Myth and Symbol in the Bible and Literature*, Crossman Publishing, 1982, p. ix.

3   Ginzberg, *Legends of the Jews*

4   Ginzberg, *Legends of the Jews*

5   References for Jesus in the boat include Matthew 8:23–27; Mark 4:35–41; Luke 8:22–25. See also Matthew 14:22–33; Mark 6:45–52; John 6:16–21.

∞

CHAPTER SEVEN

Presentation matters

The Dormouse slowly opened his eyes...
'Tell us a story!' said the March Hare.
'Yes, please do!' pleaded Alice.
'And be quick about it,' added the Hatter,
'or you'll be asleep again before it's done.'

LEWIS CARROLL, *ALICE IN WONDERLAND*, 1993 EDITION PUBLISHED
BY BRIMAX BOOKS LTD, P. 64.

It has been said that the most important preparation for beginning to tell stories is to choose a story you like, and tell it... and tell it again. Then go on telling until the love and the lure of the shared experience becomes part of who you are. I believe this is true. I also understand that whatever encouragement enables a person to *begin* telling stories, there does come a time when taking the next step of reflecting upon the process becomes appropriate.

As the Hatter in the quote above suggests, it is important to pay attention to the pacing of a story, as well as to our individual patterns of movement and speech. There are as many 'right ways' to tell a story as there are tellers. None the less, the perfect piece of material, carefully chosen and well learned, can be lost in an individual's throat or thrown away with aimless body movements. A story shared is a visual as well as an aural/oral experience. An increase of communication follows from attention to some basic details.

In this section, we will try to draw out some *principles for presentation* by exploring various techniques for:

❖ finding your voice
❖ using your body

Finding your voice

'Heigh-hey, O,' calls out the teller.

'Heigh-hey, O,' responds the group.

The teller repeats and extends the pattern until finally the sing-song game ends in laughter. Through this call and response invitation, the group is drawn together and the teller's leadership is established. The teller's voice is warmed up and all attention is focused on the story about to be told.

Experimenting with the effective practice of other storytellers is one good way to develop our own voices and style. My introduction to this interactive pattern for beginning a storytelling event came in West Africa. I was a university student, sharing in a church-sponsored voluntary work-camp experience in Ghana. The story-teller in the village where I was living began his telling with this call and response invitation. All the people knew the songs and hand-claps he used throughout his telling. As I followed their lead, it drew me more intimately into the group and allowed me to feel really part of the event. Now I understand that it helped the teller, as well as focused attention on the story he was about to tell. All these years later, I use the pattern also.

It really works. Why not try it out for yourself?

Find a call

❖ First choose a phrase or pattern of sounds you might call out to get the attention of a friend. Experiment by calling several sounds out loud.
❖ Now give your pattern a rhythm.
❖ How does it sound if you vary the pitch?

Remember that the call is meant to draw people in, not scare people away. 'Come on in!' is spoken differently from 'Get out of here!'

When you've found something you are comfortable with, take the next step.

Introduce the call in a session
First tell your listeners what you're going to do and invite them to join in. You might use something like the following dialogue. Such a pattern could be appropriate for introducing a Bible story as well as a tale from a secular or literary source. I often begin my stories about Anansi, as well as the one about David and Goliath, by saying:

'I'd like to invite you to join me on an adventure. The story for today will take us into a new place. It might be fun… it might be scary. If we get separated, we'll need to have a way to come together. When I call out to you, will you call back to me? Let's practise.'

Next, call out your phrase or sounds. I place my hand next to my mouth and call out in a sing-song rhythm, 'Heigh-ho'. When they respond, do it again… a bit differently. For example, the second call from me might be, 'Heigh-hey-ho'. The third time, extend the pattern. After the response comes, the next call might be 'Heigh-oh, heigh-oh, heigh… ho'. Try to draw the last phrase out longer than the others. Depending on the way the group responds, you can either continue for a phrase or two—going faster and faster until it all ends in laughing—or choose to stop there. Each time it is likely to be different.

Bring the game to a clear end. When the last response has been called out, sit or stand very still for a moment. Hold the silence and focus on the story you are about to share. Wait until you sense that you have the full attention of the group and that the moment to continue is right. Then begin your telling.

This little game of vocal 'follow my leader' gives you an opportunity to warm up your voice and to experiment with the acoustics in the room or hall. It offers the opportunity to test how loudly you need to speak to catch the attention of the back row of listeners and to see what happens when you speak very quietly to them as well. You can begin to see how the listeners are likely to respond and perhaps even to identify one or two who would be willing to play a fuller part in the telling.

Explore your vocal range

It is an advantage to you as storyteller to be able to vary the pitch of your voice. Changing pitch is a signal that there is action in the story. It serves continually to recapture the attention of the listener and signals interchanges between characters. Sometimes, assigning a particular voice to main characters in a story brings them more fully alive. While this technique is to be applied with discipline, it does permit a dialogue to develop between the characters and offers the listener a first-person presence to the drama. Even without the use of props, the listener can thus be invited to interact more fully with the development of the drama.

However you choose to vary the presentation of stories in your repertoire, an awareness of your own vocal characteristics is useful.
❖ How broad is your vocal range?
❖ How flexible is your voice?

When you have some time and space to yourself, you might explore what you can do. Begin by finding a comfortable place to stand or sit. Loosen your head, shoulders, limbs and torso. Take one or two deep breaths through the nose and exhale through the mouth. Select a syllable, like KEE or BAA or MOO. Speak it out loud in an ordinary voice, then try to move up and down the scale.
❖ How high can you speak?
❖ How low can you go?

Extend your arms over your head to see if it extends your range. Bend at the waist, or even get down on your hands and knees to discover a possible lower voice. What happens if you repeat the syllables quickly and then slowly?

Just for the fun of it, pretend that there are all kinds of sounds hidden in the room where you are. Move around and see if you can 'catch' some of them; speak them out as you do. There might be very high, squeaky sounds above the curtains or on top of the bookcase. Some middle-range sounds might be hiding behind the telephone or on the window-sill. Something very low might be hiding under the sofa or behind the door. Let your voice follow your playful imagination and see what happens. Presumably no one else is looking—or listening!

With your creativity warmed up, we might try something else. It is important to consider the whole personality of a character in a story in order to apply an appropriate voice. Do any of the sounds you've been playing with suggest characters? Might they be coming from large or small animals? Old or young individuals? A woman? A man? A child? Once you've matched a voice and a character, extend it a bit more. How would the character sound if they were happy or sad? Excited or bored to death? Strong or weak? Could you speak so that the character would sound very attractive, then change the voice to make the character sound threatening?

Now try to develop a simple exchange between two of your characters. A dialogue of greeting might begin:

Character 1: 'Hello.'
Character 2: 'Hello. How are you?'
Character 1: 'I'm fine. How are you?'

Allow yourself to play with the different voices. Be free to let the characters speak to each other and see what happens. How do they express their individual personalities? Can you let them have an argument? Be tender with each other? Can they 'be on the same side', as it were, and together drive off an enemy?

Now choose a story with which you are familiar and try to apply these same skills to the characters in the story. Perhaps the characters you've been expressing have already brought a story to mind. Some possible practice people might be Little Red Riding

Hood and the Wolf or the Gingerbread Man and the Fox. Could the exchange between David and Goliath be told like this? (1 Samuel 17:41–51). Or the dialogue between Mary and the angel in the story of the annunciation? (Luke 1:26–38). One Ghanaian story I like to tell is about Anansi the spider and the Lion: their interchanges lend themselves very well to a wide range of vocal characteristics.

The challenge for the storyteller is to be able to identify and maintain the different characterizations appropriately throughout the presentation. Thoughtful preparation and practice 'out loud' helps to prevent confusion. It also helps to avoid the disaster of putting the right words in the wrong character's mouth. For some examples of how others use different voices effectively, try a visit to the library to sample the audio tapes.

Listen to others

Listening to the way other people use their voices can be helpful in improving the effectiveness of our own voice production. In day-to-day conversation we express our feelings, attitudes and emotional and physical well-being as we automatically vary the pitch, rhythm and volume of our voices. The changing sound of our voices as well as the language of the body are elements of shared communication through which we unconsciously send and process social clues: stay away! come closer! I like you (or don't like you)! this is the way I feel about that! All these different pieces of information can be conveyed with body language and vocal cues.

Developing a critical attentiveness to the sound of the voices in conversation is one way to foster the flexibility of our own voices. Here are some exercises which you might try.

1. Tune in to a telly 'soap' and listen with your eyes closed. By listening to the voices alone, can you identify the hero or heroine? the troublemaker? the one who is in trouble? the family friend? a pseudo friend? the role that other characters play in the drama? What are the specific vocal characteristics which helped you to recognize these distinctions?

2. Listen to a different news programme from usual. Compare the voices of the presenters with those of your preferred broadcasters. What do you notice about the individual attributes? Do the sounds of the voices have anything to do with your preference? Make a list of the different vocal characteristics. Which ones do you like? Which ones do you dislike? Which of the commentators speaks with the more favourable balance?

3. Tune in to a radio or television chat show or round-table discussion. Listen to the voices of the speakers. Do you find yourself drawn to the point of view they express because of the sound of their voice? Are you repelled by what someone is saying by the way they sound? Would any of these terms apply to individual speakers: agreeable, irritable, pompous, antagonistic, aggressive, indifferent, conciliatory, uncertain, directive, insincere, energetic, weary, complaining, soft-spoken, friendly, warm, unkind, long-suffering, authoritative?

4. Listen critically to two or three of your friends. Are there any qualities of their voices which you particularly like? Are there any that you would change or adjust? Why?

5. Listen to two or three people you don't like quite so much. What do you notice about the sound of their voices? Do their voices have anything to do with your likes or dislikes?

As you reflect on the results of these last few exercises, here are some additional questions you might consider.
❖ Do any of the range of characteristics listed in exercise 3 above apply to people in the last two exercises?
❖ Do any of the voices you've listened to remind you of someone you knew as a child? Did you like or dislike them?
❖ Which characteristics would you like to claim as part of your own range of vocal expression?

Become conscious of your diction
Dee Dee Dee Dee
Tip Top Tip Top
Think Thin
Sling Slippery Snakes

Attention to the formation of sounds and words in telling stories promotes shared understanding and effective communication. A commitment to clear enunciation and the appropriate pronunciation of words is a significant discipline for the speaker. Such attention to detail indicates the speaker's appreciation of the language used. It also communicates an awareness of the needs of the listener.

As improving storytellers, we need to be able to evaluate whether we are actually communicating the meaning we intend through the words and gestures we use. It no longer seems relevant to attempt to establish a common standard for speech in our culture today. The multiple dialects and language families that are represented in an ordinary listening group reflect the diversity of our community groups. While in the English language we may be said to share a broad common vocabulary, various interest groups, regional variations and local idiosyncrasies suggest a very broad commonality indeed.

It is thus particularly relevant for a teller to be able to evaluate the effectiveness of their own enunciation and choice of vocabulary. Part of the information we need comes from others. Their response will communicate whether they are receiving what we are trying to 'send'. We also need to become 'self-listeners'. It is important to be able to hear our own voice patterns and to develop an awareness of the ways we end and begin words. There is considerable evidence to show that learning to listen to our own voices is helpful in the improvement of both voice and diction. Here are some questions which might help develop a self-listening checklist:

❖ Is the listening group responding as I expect? Does their response show they are following the story?

❖ Am I speaking at the right level and speed for my words to come out clearly in the way I intend? Would it be easier to tell the story if I spoke more slowly or speeded up a bit?

❖ Am I getting the volume right for the venue and the group? Am I speaking too quietly or dropping the sound at the end of my sentences?
❖ Do the voices I try to give to different characters work effectively? Next time, should I change the pitch or rhythm?
❖ How does my throat feel when I'm finished?
❖ Do my breathing patterns seem normal when I'm telling? Do I have enough breath to enjoy the telling or does it seem that I'm short of breath?

Recognize good breathing habits[1]

A relaxed and flexible speaking voice for the storyteller depends upon good breathing. Good breathing for speaking is that which provides a sufficient and comfortable supply of breath. One characteristic of good breathing for speaking is when the intake and exhalation of the breath is accomplished smoothly, almost automatically. Good breathing doesn't interfere with the pattern of speech. Properly supported, such breathing requires little expenditure of effort and does not draw attention to the process.

In most cases, good breathing for storytelling is sustained by the almost unconscious practice of abdominal breath control. In this pattern, the muscles of the abdomen relax in inhalation and contract in exhalation. The throat muscles do not control the breathing. Are you speaking freely? Are you using proper abdominal support?

If you're not sure what you're doing, here's a way to discover your habit. Place one hand very gently around your throat. Now speak a few sentences in an ordinary voice. If you feel any tightening of the throat muscles at all, you are not speaking freely.

To discover your pattern of breath support, place your hands on your hips with your thumbs toward the back. Inhale normally and then exhale through the mouth. If your hands rise with the diaphragm when you inhale and fall with the abdomen when you exhale, then you are breathing correctly. To correct or reinforce this pattern, here are some exercises that are easy to use.

❖ Choose a chair which allows you to sit with your feet flat on the floor, keeping your back straight. Gently clear your mind of other thoughts so that you are free to concentrate on the intake and outflow of your breath. Place your hands on your waist with the thumbs toward the back. Inhale through your nose and exhale through your mouth. Allow your abdominal muscles to push forward as you inhale and pull in as you exhale. Repeat once or twice until this seems to happen easily.

❖ As you continue this pattern, try to slow down the intake of breath somewhat—inhaling for about five seconds—and to sustain the length of exhalation. If you run out of breath before ten seconds, you may be exhaling too quickly. As you repeat this pattern, press down gently but firmly on the abdomen to encourage the full expression of air as you exhale.

❖ Draw another breath. This time, vocalize a clear 'ah' as you exhale. Start the 'ah' as soon as you begin to exhale. Repeat, switching to a 'hmm' sound as you continue to exhale. Do you notice that the exhalation lasts longer when you are making a sound?

❖ Now let your hands fall to your sides, and try counting as you exhale. You will probably be able to count to almost twenty on one exhalation. Experiment with different patterns of counting. For example, count 1, 2, 3, 4... pause... continue 5, 6, 7, 8 and so on. Now try again, pausing in a different place. Can you 'phrase' your counting easily and continue without drawing breath? Are you becoming more aware of when you need to allow the next intake of breath?

❖ As you try this again, switch to saying the alphabet instead of numbers. Allow the pitch and rhythm of your voice to vary as you speak. You might try to simulate a pattern of 'conversation' between two different speakers as you go through the alphabet.

Here is a list of sentences and quotations to read. Read them singly and then in pairs. If you cannot read the longer ones in a single breath, try to draw your breath so that what you are saying still makes sense.

An honest tale speeds best being plainly told.

SHAKESPEARE, *RICHARD III*

A good story cannot be devised; it has to be distilled.

RAYMOND CHANDLER, *RAYMOND CHANDLER SPEAKING*, 1962

I am always at a loss to know how much to believe of my own stories.

WASHINGTON IRVING, *TALES OF A TRAVELLER*

There are only two or three human stories, and they go on repeating themselves as fiercely as if they had never happened before.

WILLA CATHER, *O PIONEERS!* 1913

I have tried to remove weight, sometimes from people, sometimes from heavenly bodies, sometimes from cities; above all I have tried to remove weight from the structure of stories and from language.

ITALO CALVINE (1923–1985), *SIX MEMOS FOR THE NEXT MILLENNIUM*

Singers and actors receive training in good breathing and clear enunciation. To carry your own exploration and development further, a church music director or drama teacher at the local school might be able to offer relevant local opportunities.

Using the body

Taking a stand

The decision to stand or sit during a story presentation is a matter of personal preference. None the less, an effective choice needs to be based on the elements of the venue and the listening group as well as on the physical needs of the teller. While either choice *can* be translated into an appropriate presentation for a given event, some venues strongly suggest one pattern of presentation over another. Both positions may be employed by a given teller to vary the presentation of a longer programme or adapt the telling to the changing demands of a given situation.

Whichever pattern you select in the moment, here are two or three questions which usually serve as reliable reference points for making the decision.

Can you keep the whole listening group within your field of vision? Be aware that the teller's line of sight extends out like a triangle in front of you. Those people sitting outside that triangle are, by default, excluded from the group. If you have chosen to sit, and find, as the listening group is finally assembled, that some are beyond your sight line, stand up and step back or move your seat back. Make the necessary adjustments before you begin in order that all may be comfortable.

Are you physically close enough to the listening group for there to be a corporate sense of shared space? The distance between the teller and the listeners is significant. Too close and only those near you are included; too far away and the presentation becomes more of a performance, too impersonal for individual involvement. When working in a school or telling stories with groups in a library, I usually prefer to sit on a low chair with children sitting on the floor around me. Standing in front of a small group seated on the floor increases the physical and psychological distance between us.

Likewise, when working in a large hall with only a small number of people, it is usually preferable to sit. By choosing a seated position with my back to the wall, near one corner of the room, even a large gymnasium can offer an intimate space for telling. Placing chairs for adult listeners just behind the floor-seated children can also help to define and personalize a large open area.

Can the listeners easily see you—the teller? There are some situations where a seated teller can become lost to the listening group. Fixed seating for the listeners, in rows or around tables, limits individual sight lines. Such limitations make it more difficult for the listener to feel an integrated part of the programme. Each listener needs to be able easily to see at least the face, arms and upper torso of the teller. In such situations, it is usually most effective for the teller to stand. If the teller must sit, a tall stool or pedestal chair can help bring the teller into view. A small platform may also improve the teller's visibility.

When 'telling' to a group seated around tables, offer them an opportunity to turn their chairs before beginning. It is as important for you to have eye contact as for them to be able to see you clearly. Feel free to make the necessary adjustments before introducing the story. You may be able to make a bit of a joke about this preparation and warm the group to you before you even begin.

Descriptive movement

Choose the movements you make with your body with great care. Allow your gestures, facial expressions and change of position to come naturally. The one point of reference is that they must be in the service of the story. Specific gestures may help to draw the listener in, to give shape to elements of the story, or to dramatize the movements of characters. Random hand and arm movements and unconscious pacing distract the listener and intrude upon the story material.

Hand and arm movements

It is useful to begin your telling with your hands and arms in a neutral position. If seated, with both feet resting comfortably on the floor and sitting with back straight, let your hands rest in your lap. Beware of sinking into a comfy chair with legs crossed and arms folded. If you have chosen to stand, begin with your arms and hands in a relaxed position at your side. Folded arms, clasped hands, and hands stuffed in pockets diminish rather than enhance the presentation.

Body movements

Sometimes it's hard to stand still. It becomes a bit of a discipline to stand in the 'telling space' and wait while the listeners enter the room and settle. It is often preferable to sit or stand to one side and then walk into the 'telling space' when it is time to begin the telling.

Giving some thought to how you will move in the space can improve the presentation. While you may not be inclined to plan a full choreography for your telling, having a sense of when and to which position you might move is significant. If the space is small, turning your head may be more effective than moving from place to place.

Integrating previous exercises

In Chapter Three, 'Stepping into the story', we have already explored some of the positive ways body movement contributes to the preparation of material for telling. Revisiting these exercises might suggest movement or placing which can be adapted for telling the story. Perhaps a characteristic gesture or stance discovered while moving through the story can be used to help identify a character. Ideas for standing, or sitting, or moving from one part of the telling area to another, might also come from these exercises.

Likewise, a gesture can be effectively used in a 'follow my leader' responsive way with the listening group. Such play can serve to invite movement and physical activity, thus allowing a deeper level of listening to be maintained. In a way similar to the vocal call and response game at the beginning of this chapter, signs and gestures can also be used effectively throughout a story. The actions and sounds of the different fish, animals and winged creatures in the story of creation may be 'assigned' to different sections of a large listening group and invited as response at the appropriate time of the telling. Likewise, actions for the animals in the story of Noah's ark can also be invited from the listening group in order to draw everyone safely in from the rain. Even better ideas for similar applications have probably already begun to occur to you.

NOTES

1 Points in this section take particular notice of the work of Barbara Alden. Her chapter on 'Singing', pp. 13–16 in *The Choral Singers' Companion* by Ronald Corp, is particularly helpful. It was first published by Batsford, 1987, and is due to be re-published by Kevin Mayhew.

∞

CHAPTER EIGHT

Props and people

> *Your hands create my body*
> *your mouth breathes life in me*
> *my face shines in your eyes*
> *you call me by my name.*
> *Alone how should I shine?*

FROM 'GENESIS' BY EVA TÓTH (TRANSLATED FROM THE HUNGARIAN),
MODERN POEMS ON THE BIBLE: AN ANTHOLOGY ED. DAVID CURZON,
THE JEWISH PUBLICATION SOCIETY, 1994, P. 55.

Ezekiel tells the story that the hand of the Lord set him down in a valley of dry bones. When he prophesied to the bones what God had told him, sinews and flesh and skin came upon the bones. Breath came into them; they stood on their feet and lived (Ezekiel 37:1–14). When we give voice to the stories we have chosen and prepared, they too take flesh and begin to come alive. They come alive in our hearts and imaginations as well as in the minds and hearts of our listeners.

The creative and controlled use of props and people can enhance and extend the comprehension and interactive enjoyment of a story told. Such work earths the narrative in a very tangible way. It provides a visual focus for the shared oral material. It stimulates people's mental processes with the use of form, shape, colour and movement. It takes advantage of the psychological dynamics of transitional objects to help people move and to explore new ideas and understanding.

Such an invitation to play releases energy and invites a new group sense of direction and fun. When applied to a programme for young children, it enables understanding and participation, sometimes even across language barriers. When implemented in a presentation for adults, the use of props and people tends to strengthen a sense of corporate fellowship and suggests possible connections for further development. Used to present a story in the middle of an experience of worship, such an approach can provide an effective transition space for deeper involvement with what comes after. Used to present the last story in a programme, the new energy and building sense of fun can provide a memorable and fun-filled finish. It is not unusual for a story presented with 'props and people' to draw the heartiest and healthiest laughter in an entire programme.

In this section I will offer tips and techniques for:

❖ setting background materials
❖ introducing props
❖ interacting with puppets
❖ inviting members of the 'listening group' to take part

Setting background materials

Pay attention to the environment

What the listener sees, around and behind the storyteller, affects to some degree what the listener hears. What lies in the storyteller's field of vision is also significant. When you are setting up a story-telling space, be aware of the nature and placement of the objects and furniture. Notice how the light source will affect both the listeners and the teller. Anticipate where there could be potential movement or other distracting activity outside the group space during the event.

Use the ordinary features of the environment to help integrate the story with the event. Furniture and fixtures associated with a particular venue can provide a natural focus for a story. The same story presented at the pub, in a school library, or in a local church might be expected to have a slightly different natural emphasis depending on the environment in which it is told. The sensitive teller can make use of the venue, the surrounding objects and visible symbols to focus the attention of the listener and promote understanding.

The sensitive teller will also be aware of likely background activity. People coming and going through an open door or across an open space can be very distracting to a group's attention. External exits and entrances do not usually distract the listener's attention when they happen out of sight. Latecomers and early leavers can be accommodated from a position at the back of the group without disturbing the listeners' attention. Pints can be pulled, books can be checked out, and wardens can prepare for what is coming next if the activities happen out of the listeners' sight lines.

Carefully choose the space for the listeners

Be aware that the space to be occupied by the listeners has several requirements. It needs to be spacious enough to accommodate all who might come. Preparation for a potential group of listeners in a smaller library setting or a space for story hour in a classroom includes a 'guess-timate' of the numbers expected. Containers of books might need to be shifted for the event; tables and chairs might need to be moved. It is important that everyone be able to sit comfortably in their own space, and usually preferable for all to be similarly accommodated. Make provisions for special needs and differences when necessary. If a group of children are to be seated on the floor, chairs can be provided at the side or back for adults.

Telling stories in large open places involves limiting the space appropriately. In a school hall or gymnasium, a chair for the teller, side chairs for adult listeners, and perhaps a back row of benches, can help to claim the area for the size of group expected. In an open-air setting, spreading out a carpet or tracing a good-sized circle on the ground with a length of thick cord can effectively define a listening space.

Large spaces with fixed seating, like churches and auditoriums, can present a challenge if a small group is expected. Inviting a more intimate atmosphere might be done by placing a good-sized rug or ring of movable chairs in an open space, or defining one area of the fixed seating with bows or balloons. Claiming the space in advance is part of the invitation to the listener to 'enter' the whole experience.

Remember that the position of the teller is significant

Identifying the position of the teller in relation to the listening group contributes to the nature of the shared experience. One central 'speaker's position' in front of rows of designated seating for 'listeners' suggests the outline of an experience quite different from that defined by a circle of chairs with the storyteller's place as 'one among many'. Attendance numbers and visibility lines may determine the more appropriate choices. You need to be conscious of the extent to which an event is to be a performance versus a shared telling, and prepare the environment accordingly.

Your choice, as teller, to either stand or sit also influences the atmosphere of the group. It is usually preferable to choose to stand or sit in front of a wall or fixed backdrop. Even when the group is sitting in a circle, a stable background helps to free the listener's attention to be focused on the teller and on the unfolding of the tale itself. When it is possible for you to choose where to be placed and how the group may be arranged, your informed choices can promote effective and attractive presentations.

Be prepared to take advantage of the unexpected

Even the most reflective choice for positioning both the listeners and the tellers will never entirely eliminate all distractions and spontaneous interventions. The decision to integrate or ignore such moments will continue to challenge tellers and delight listeners. Such an unexpected intervention can sometimes provide a memorable shared moment for the whole group.

One such memorable moment clings to the Harvest Sunday, in my home church, when I was invited to tell a story during the sermon spot. This particular all-age worship service is traditionally well attended by the whole community and that year was no exception—the pews were comfortably full. The entire church was decorated in tribute to the fruitfulness and generosity of a loving creator God.

Baskets and bowls of fruit and vegetables and flowers seemed to blossom forth out of every available space. Crates of rabbits, and hens; ferrets, ducks and hamsters from the local city farm were strategically placed in the chancel area. The local service organizations were well represented and banners and flags had been presented and displayed. The place for me to stand was very clearly defined.

I stepped into this space and began my story. People were responsive; laughter and focused listening were offered in the right places. As the telling continued, we all appeared to be drawn into the safe and sacred space that the narrative was offering. When the story reached its climax, there was a very tangible moment of deep silence and connectedness which the whole group seemed to be savouring. After holding the silence for a moment or two, I spread my arms wide and leaned forward, offering the group a deep bow to express my gratitude for their response and to bring that part of the service to a close.

With a precision that no amount of rehearsal or training could have produced, the ducks in the cages behind me, who had remained quite still throughout the telling of the story, broke into a loud, raucous and sustained chorus of quacking. There was no holding the outpouring of surprise and goodnatured laughing which came from the congregation. The detail of the narrative may not be long remembered but the fancy finish with a chorus of ducks is annually recalled. For me it gave truth to the piece of Hebrew *midrash* which suggests that God created human beings in the first place in order to be able to share a good joke.

Introducing props

While a story well told provides its own attractions, the introduction of simple props can help you to focus attention and give tangible shape to oral material. Traditional ornaments and characteristic objects displayed in the storytelling area provide valuable clues to the environment of tales from other lands and cultures. Wall hangings of texture and colour help to stimulate the atmosphere and set the tone for a particular story. The symbols and spaces in a worship setting serve to lead both teller and listener into the sacred space of God's story shared.

Be selective

Choose artefacts and props which help to focus attention on the story to be told. Since the story itself defines a space in which individuals add their own perceived details, it is counter-productive to introduce objects which themselves become the focus of attention. Be sensitive to the number of props you use in a story and the frequency with which you introduce them in your work. 'Less is more' is usually a helpful adage. Fewer props also means less baggage for the itinerant storyteller to carry!

Use with care

Once you have decided to use an object, make sure it is carefully introduced and just as carefully returned to its keeping place at the end of a story. Random or careless handling of objects creates a distraction for the group. Props or puppets which take on personalities in the telling need to be carefully retired; this is a mark of respect for the listening group and their feelings, as much as for the care of the prop. Objects casually discarded after one story become distractions if another story or activity is to follow.

Let the story suggest the prop

To introduce a harvest story, you might present a large pumpkin, or lean on a crook to begin one of the shepherd narratives. A crown, or even a baby blanket, could be used with many different pieces of material. An instrument or piece of music might also be included and lead from one story to another. Introducing additional arte-facts throughout can even help to vary the mood and pace in a longer programme.

It isn't always the story that gets chosen first. Sometimes a particularly attractive ornament will speak to a teller in such a way that it sparks the preparation of a new piece of material. The purchase of a particularly attractive pair of 'mud cloths' from Africa prompted me to increase my repertoire of stories and songs and poems from different parts of that continent. The sight of a beautiful crystal box in a museum helped me in the preparation and presentation of a folk tale, even though I have never had such a box to display. (For a fuller telling of that particular story, refer to page 55, 'An imagined tale'.)

Involve the listeners

The listeners can use the props, too. People enjoy sharing new ways to present familiar material and are stimulated to try out their own retelling. To introduce one particular Bible story, I pass five large stones around the group. After giving the listeners time to have a close look at the stones and to get the feel of them, I invite them to 'switch on their imaginations' and to wonder what stories those stones could tell if they could talk. My questions include:

❖ How long do you think these stones have been around?
❖ Where do you think they might have been carried?
❖ What adventures do you think they might have survived?

After receiving the replies, I suggest that I have a Bible story to share which one of the stones might tell if it could talk. Have you already guessed what story it is? This is how my retelling begins.

Hi. I'm Rocky. And this is my sister Pebbles. [N.B. It can just as easily be told the other way round!] We were just lying around in the river bed one day when this kid came by and picked us up. He stuffed us in a bag with three other stones and we bounced around together for a while. When he pulled me out of the bag, I could hardly believe what I saw. You may find it hard to believe, too, when

I tell you what happened next. The boy's name was David. He wasn't very old but he turned out to be a big hero.

By now I'm sure it's clear that this is a possible start for a retelling of the encounter between David and Goliath found in 1 Samuel 17. I've found this to be an effective presentation and often offer my listeners an opportunity to retell the story themselves, holding the stone, of course. (For further development of the ideas related to stories suggested by objects, refer to Chapter One, 'Story starts with simple things' also Chapter Four, 'The Bag of Bags and the stories inside'.)

Interacting with puppets

Within the repertoire of the storyteller, puppets have a place. Sensitively used, they can help to focus attention and contribute to pace and atmosphere. Allowed to become an end in themselves, they can divert the teller's energies and the listeners' attention away from interaction with the story itself. While the art and craft of puppetry is a discipline in its own right, the intention of this section is to highlight some of the possible uses of puppets in telling stories.

Puppets can offer an additional 'voice'

Enlivened with movement, personality and 'voice', a puppet can become a storytelling companion. The face-to-face dialogue which develops is somewhat different to the relationship between a puppet and the puppeteer who provides these gifts from behind a screen or black drape. The interaction between the storyteller and the puppet is also different from that between a ventriloquist and their companion. The listening group's creative identification will happily allow the puppet to speak for itself, even when the teller's mouth is moving.

Neither is it necessary for the puppet and the teller to advocate the same point of view. In practice, the puppet can speak or behave in a way which the teller might find inappropriate. The tension created between a teller and a puppet with opposing points of view can be a creative stimulus for unfolding challenging and/or scary stories. Several of the *BabaYaga* stories from Russian folklore lend themselves to such a telling... and the teller can choose the appropriate role to occupy. Bible stories can be successfully told in dialogue with puppets as well. The puppet might be a child (or children) who sees things in a particular way, or an adult who may or may not always have the right answers.

What ideas occur to you? How about a dialogue between a disciple and the child who offered his lunch? (John 6:9). Or maybe one between Jesus and the disciples about who could come close to him (Mark 10:13–16). As storyteller, from which role would you choose to speak? One American supplier of Christian books and materials offers a Jesus doll. This doll has proved to be a faithful companion for sharing Bible stories with younger children and in all-age worship events.

Hand puppets are very accessible

The most basic hand puppet is worn almost like a glove and operated with one, two or three fingers. It can usually move its arms, head and body. It can look to left and right, bow and bend, pick things up, and run or even fly. As with all puppets, when presenting the character it is important that every movement should have a meaning. Even hand puppets that are created as specific characters can be used in a storytelling programme in a variety of ways. Although the dialogue with the puppet can offer a controversial point of view that neither the storyteller nor another member of the listening group would own, that isn't always the case.

During one event in a long-stay unit in a local hospital, the puppet in my bag of tricks really saved the programme. It was the first time I'd been to share stories in such a situation. There were perhaps 20 residents/patients in the listening group and I'd been invited to offer a programme of stories lasting 45 minutes. I had been telling stories for about half an hour and in spite of all my best efforts, we simply did not seem to be communicating.

The people in the listening group seemed content enough to be there. They were sitting in pairs or close together, and even the ones sitting more on their own were reacting from time to time—they just didn't seem to be reacting to the stories I was telling. There was laughter and some background conversation but even the follow-my-leader calling games and props I'd used hadn't really involved the whole group. In desperation, I drew a hand puppet resembling a grandmother figure from my bag, placed her on my hand, and spoke to her.

'I'm having a very difficult day, grandmother. Things just aren't going the way I expected them to.'

'I understand,' was her reply. 'I don't know why things like this happen, but just keep going. Why don't you finish by telling the story of the special pot? I'll help you.'

It was almost as if a hush fell over the listening group. For the first time they were really absorbed in what I was doing. The granny puppet and I told the story of the special pot, a retelling of a family story my mother-in-law had often shared with me, and the response from the group was very positive. I drew the story out as long as I could, and then brought the session to a close. I was so relieved that we'd come together at last.

Later, in the staff room, I spoke with the nurse/therapist who had invited me along. When I asked her to help me figure out why the group responded as they did, her insight opened up a whole new area of understanding for me. 'They all have voices, too,' was her reply. 'And the ones that speak inside their heads are usually not so understanding. Maybe when the group heard the kindness in your puppet's voice, they were drawn to what was happening.' I did return, several times, and grandmother puppet always came along, too.

Your fingers and hand can become a puppet

In finger play and rhyming games, a rabbit or a caterpillar or even an 'eensy-weensy spider' can crawl out of the teller's hand. Such interactive games with a very young listening group are fun, and help to focus the group. Your hand, folded with a moving thumb on the bottom, can also become a puppet. Such a puppet is able to turn its head from side to side, look around and open and close its mouth. Because of that, it's often called a 'mouth puppet'. Adding some colour to the mouth and a scarf or small cap, even a bit of hair to the top of the hand, can give this character an even more distinctive identity.

Another possible 'mouth puppet' can be formed by pulling a sock over your hand. Margie Brown, a storyteller *extraordinaire*— especially in her clown character—would sit down and remove her sock to make such a puppet. She then proceeded to share an absorbing and very moving retelling of the Song of Songs. Facial features and different hair and head coverings can be added to such sock puppets, but then it's more difficult to wear them!

For a puppet of this type, your own hand or fist provides all the movements. It is particularly important to synchronize these movements so the puppet's speech is visually effective—open hand for vowels, closed mouth for consonants. For example, just to practise, let your fingers and thumb become a mouth puppet reciting the nursery rhyme 'Baa Baa Black Sheep...' Does it work? Do you see how important it is to exaggerate these movements so that the character really spits out the words? When the puppet is not talking, it should be held still. Movement goes with speech for a mouth puppet.

Shadow puppets can have a modern-day application

Shadow puppets may have been around when cave dwellers sat around their home fires, but moving hands and fingers in front of a light to cast shadows on a wall or ceiling can still be a very dramatic illustration in a story. The accessibility of overhead pro-jectors can make this type of puppetry an option in a variety of settings. It is a natural step to move from words on a screen to introducing characters and shapes which move in the same space. In both classroom and worship settings, it is possible to introduce shadow puppets to help tell a story. When the story follows group singing, the puppets and the teller are able to capitalize on the eye contact and rapport already established with even quite a large group of listeners.

Try telling the story of Jacob wrestling with the angel (Genesis 32:22–26) with shadow puppets: the shapes and the movement between them are more significant than bodily or facial characteristics. A retelling of Jesus' parable of the mustard seed might also work well in this medium (Matthew 13:31–32). Something which, to begin with, appears on the screen to be very small could in fact be constructed to unroll in such a way that many birds of the air could fly in to find nesting-places there.

Rod puppets are easy to use

The simplest puppets of individual figures on a single rod can be visually useful with a group and easy for a storyteller to use. They might be as basic as a drawing or picture cut out and mounted on a stick. When used close up with a small group, the detail of the figure could help to set the scene and indicate the natural environment of the character. Copies of such a resource might be duplicated as a possible follow-up bit of work, should members of the listening group want to retell the story themselves. (See Chapter Nine, 'Open to wonder', for a fuller discussion of this in practice.)

A 'three-dimensional' toy or stuffed animal mounted in such a way to make it movable and visible can be a very useful rod puppet. In fact, more than one such puppet might be shared out among members of the listening group to encourage an interactive telling. (See the section that follows for additional suggestions about inviting members of the listening group to take part.)

Giant rod puppets have some very special applications. During one festival celebration in Hereford Cathedral, a local school presented giant puppets to help in the telling of the Bible readings for the event. As individual giant rod puppets of Jesus and his friends moved into the space, people throughout the packed cathedral were able to see the characters and watch their interactive movements as the story was told. Perhaps this is more than one person can manage alone, yet it serves to highlight the corporate nature of the story-sharing experience. Such a sharing is always composed of the listeners and the teller, and all are drawn in to become part of the tale itself as the story unfolds.

Inviting members of the 'listening group' to take part

Offering people props to hold or inviting them into the teller's space to play a part can be fun for the listener and interesting for the whole group. The maintenance of continuity and leadership is the responsibility of the teller. The available space grows out of a developed relationship between the listeners and the teller. In a longer programme, such a relationship builds throughout the time together; in a single story offering, the teller must establish control from the beginning. The exercise serves to deepen group ident-ification with the story itself.

Patterns of use

There are different ways to involve people in the telling. These vary according to the tale itself, the size and profile of the group, the length of the programme, or the disposition of the teller. You might choose to use more than one approach in a longer programme to help vary the pace and level of involvement. With appropriate introduction and group management, I have found each of the following patterns widely applicable, even in traditionally quite formal settings.

Whole group response

I like to establish rapport and direct communication, even with quite a large group, from the very beginning. I might begin by saying 'hello' and indicating or waiting for a reply from them. Such a pattern of group echo or mime can be used in various ways within a given story and throughout a longer programme. I might even suggest to the listeners that they 'switch on' their imagination or in some other way focus on what we will be doing together.

Sometimes I call to them with a word or phrase or even a series of notes, and invite them to repeat or echo my call. Often I will establish such a rhythm or sung phrase as a way of introducing one story and subsequently linking it to another. (Refer to Chapter Seven, under 'Find a call', for a description of this exercise.)

Holding up props 'in place'

Some stories lend themselves to be told using props which can be distributed to the group and held up, or worn. This allows a number of people to participate without interrupting the flow of the material. One such story is a retelling of 'The Hat Man'. This fanciful character in the story plies his trade of selling hats... in the jungle. Sometimes I choose an individual to act the part of the Hat Man and pile the hats on top of his or her head. Alternatively, I might stack the hats on a table beside me or present them, one at a time, from out of my travelling bag.

The Hat Man in the story transports his stock by piling the hats on top of his head and wandering along the paths calling out, 'Hats for sale'. When he pauses under a tree for a nap, the monkeys who live there climb down and snatch all his hats for themselves. At this point I pass out all the hats to various members of the listening group. As the story continues, there is a repetitive series of actions that the whole group is invited to echo, and the individual hat wearers, of course, are the featured monkeys. Even quite serious-looking adults are willing to accept a hat in a mixed-age group, and children are never reluctant to accept such a featured role.

A retelling of the story of the coming of the Spirit at Pentecost and how the gifts of the Spirit were made visible among the early Church is another story which has lent itself to this approach. Identification of the different gifts may be as elaborate as distributing objects in parcels to be unwrapped by the recipient or as simple as envelopes containing words printed on cards. Often a child will happily become the Spirit sharing the gifts out among members of the Church. Such a retelling tends to draw a group or congregation together, and offers quite a tangible experience. Some very happy and moving experiences have been shared as the gifts, when opened, have been found to be placed very appropriately throughout the group.

Accepting a role 'up front'

Some stories lend themselves to a series of players and a variety of defining bits of costume or props. For singles or pairs of performers, they can occupy a position either side of the teller. For larger group 'productions', a performance space must be cleared and the teller should assume a leading position to one side. The story of 'The House that Jack Built' has become a favourite, with its string of identifiable characters and some very imaginative bits of costume for the cat and the rat (not to mention the sack of malt). 'The Wise and Foolish Builders' (Matthew 7:24–27) can be told with a similar group.

The story of Noah and the ark also tells well with this approach (Genesis 6—9). Hats and ties and wigs and aprons can happily identify Noah and Mrs Noah and the sons and their wives. God can have a special hat, or wear a crown, or even speak from behind a cloth or cloud. Words and phrases can be fed to the players from the teller. The teller as narrator holds the story together and keeps the action flowing.

In the Noah story, the whole listening group can be invited to participate. The coming down of the rain, the increase of the storm, and the return to quiet suggest a Mexican Wave-like action which can be passed along rows or around a circle. Likewise, when it's time for the animals to enter the ark, even the members of a good-sized group can pair up, choose some identifying behaviour, and make their way through the door of an imaginary ark.

Tips for trying it

The opportunity to rehearse such possible approaches with a group often depends upon the kindness of a teller's family or friends. It is useful to try out one small experiment of new material within a longer programme which is familiar. Don't lose control of a good story-sharing by trying to introduce too many new ideas too soon.

This handful of helpful hints might serve you as a guide until you develop your own rules of thumb.

Choose props to share that are simple and easy to use/wear

If the props are complicated to use or the pieces of costume difficult to put on, the rhythm of the telling becomes lost and the group is distracted. Hats, ties and cloaks are easy to put on. Stuffed animals, simple figures on a large card and objects with no moving parts are good props to share. They can be passed out to group members and collected at the end with little fuss.

Connect the props to the story and the people to the props

Be sure that the props you use grow out of the story itself. My collection of hats can be used to retell several different stories, but the props I use for telling the story of Moses and Aaron and the contest with Pharaoh are specific indeed (Exodus 7—12). In such a long story, it can be an advantage to offer several different people the opportunity to hold the prop or speak the part of the main characters. It's also a feature of such imaginative play that gendered roles can be shared between both boys and girls.

Be sensitive to likely players

It is usually apparent who the extrovert members of the group are, who might be the most interested in being 'up front' as one of the characters in a story. Making a choice of people to use might be based upon a clearly expressed desire as well as good behaviour in a large group. It is important to spread the opportunity throughout the group according to age and gender, as well as where they are sitting. In a joint programme attended by several classes or groups of people, this is especially relevant.

Being chosen for a part values the contribution of a group member in a special way. I've frequently been told, after an event, that a child who has made an excellent contribution as a player or a mime in a story presentation finds affirmation in other areas difficult to attain.

Produce and reclaim the props with precision

A large carrying bag provides one good way to transport the necessary props as well as providing a storage place until the appropriate moment to introduce the items. Bringing individual props out of the bag, one at a time, builds anticipation as the story progresses and helps the teller to regulate pace and timing. Choosing the player and distributing the prop with care values the player as well as modelling the appropriate behaviour with the prop. Reclaiming the props from the individual with equal attention provides an opportunity to affirm the individual's contribution as well as to carefully repack the prop for later transportation.

Keep control

This is the ultimate responsibility of you as the teller. If the group is responsive and involved with the development of the tale, an extemporaneous extension of the telling can be fruitful. If the group finds it difficult to stay within the bounds of the telling, fewer 'players' and a more succinct storyline are definitely in order. Your sensitivity to the use of this approach develops with experience. Seasoned tellers know that every group is different and that each story must be adapted to specific group needs and requirements.

Have fun, too

This is one more opportunity to remind ourselves that it is entirely appropriate to really enjoy the storytelling experience. The extent to which you, the teller, are relaxed and participating in the fun of the developing event, as well as exercising the necessary leadership, communicates itself to the listeners. Your own comfort level contributes to the opportunity for the listeners to relax and enjoy themselves as well.

∞

CHAPTER NINE

Open to wonder

A bird... a bee... the sky... the sea.
All these speak of God to me.

SANDRA POLLERMAN

What catches your attention as you walk along the street on the way to the car park... the bus stop... the office.... the theatre... or church? The brilliant red berries on the neighbour's bush can often draw my attention away from the slowly moving cars belching petrol fumes into my morning's few minutes walk along the pavement. Sometimes a droplet-laden spider's web stretched between the branches of shrubbery will actually cause me to pause. Reflecting on this caused me to realize that it has been quite a long time since I actually bent down to the pavement to trace a slug's passage along the surface, or stretched full out on the grass to watch the procession of ants moving in and out of their mound.

Current researchers remind us that children have neither yet forgotten how to be open to wonder nor learned the adult discipline of overriding attention to duty and professional schedules.[1] My experience suggests that some aspect of our human memory and essential self never forgets. The objects, creatures, and actions surprising or intriguing enough to catch and hold our musing attention really are still all around each one of us in daily living. The willingness to be open to wonder is our challenge.

Children work out what they think and feel, and come to know who they are, through imagination and play.[2] Such activity offers opportunities for the interweaving of 'inner' experience and external 'reality'. This process of learning and growing requires a secure and trustworthy environment. We as adults can offer our children such an environment at home and at school, but perhaps most especially within the worshipping community where we meet regularly for celebration, for learning and for prayer. When we come alongside our children, we are invited to listen as they express their experience in play and pictures which are often more articulate than words.[3]

During a course of study, I was introduced to a pattern for religious education of young children which attempts to take these understandings seriously. 'Godly Play' is an imaginative approach to religious education with young children proposed by Jerome W. Berryman. Berryman identifies himself as an educator and says that 'Godly Play' is about religious growth and how to foster it.[4] In Berryman's approach, the role of the storyteller is the model for one of the adult leaders.

The sections in this chapter will include:
- ❖ a discussion of Godly Play
- ❖ a narrative report of a trial experience
- ❖ an unexpected 'postscript'

Godly Play: an introduction

I find much to enjoy in Berryman's work. His model seems to identify and offer points of integration for aspects of good practice with young children. His approach is formed around sharing stories from the Bible following the pattern of the worship of the Church. He proposes a total learning environment which is designed to take seriously the experiences and needs of the young child.

As Berryman focuses on the importance of learning to use the language of religion, the preparation of the learning environment is important. He understands that children learn from what they see and touch as well as from what they hear and say. Berryman offers a series of scripted retellings of the cycle of stories which he has developed over a period of time. He has also designed a set of simple figures and materials in order to implement a sensorimotor approach to telling the stories, a practice especially appropriate with young children.

Berryman recognizes imagination and play as primary gateways to this learning. The material and objects for learning are displayed in the classroom in a systematic way.

Boxes and trays which hold the figures and materials for telling the stories stand on shelves according to their use—parable boxes, boxes which contain materials for helping to tell the sacred stories, a tray of sand called a 'desert box', and so on. Paint, paper, crayons and other creative materials lie waiting in a defined area. A cross, a candle and other liturgical symbols are placed in their own special section of the room.

Two adult leaders work together to present each session. Over time, the leaders and the children can come to know each other well. One adult acts as doorkeeper. This person greets the children, and helps them to say goodbye to their parents and find a place in the circle. The other adult is the storyteller who will share the Bible story and co-ordinate the session. The storyteller waits in the space where the circle of meeting will form. When each child has been welcomed and all are settled and ready, the session continues with the telling of the story.

The plan for each session reflects the pattern of the Eucharist and follows the cycle of the Church's year. The Bible story is told in a way which invites both listener and teller to interact with the material in an authentic way. Focusing on the story which will unfold in the middle of the group, the storyteller moves the figures through the pattern of the story, modelling an involvement and attentiveness appropriate for the listener as well. Respectfully, the teller invites a series of 'wondering' questions which draw out aspects of the story and focus on individual thoughts and observations. At the end of the telling, the materials and figures are carefully returned to their appropriate containers.

In each session, a period of time is set aside for individual follow-up work. The work may be completed in one day or saved in a folder with the child's name on it for further development another time. In the Berryman model, each child is invited to choose an activity through which to respond to the material shared in the circle. One child might choose to retell the story using the same materials in their own working space. Another might choose to work with the materials of a story previously told. Another might use paint or crayons or art materials to catch their thoughts or ideas about one of the stories. At the end of the work time, materials are returned to the shelves and the children reform in a circle.

Each session ends with a time of sharing. Ideally there would be a time for the children to say something about their work or show the group what they had been doing. There would also be time for everyone to have some refreshment—usually a drink of juice and a biscuit. The session ends with a prayer and saying goodbye. The doorkeeper helps the children as they are met at the door and depart.

An application of Godly Play

An invitation

In *Young Children and Worship*, written in collaboration with Sonja Stewart, Berryman points out, '(Godly Play) enables young children to bring their lived experience into dialogue with God in the Bible stories. And, remarkably, it provides a way for young children to tell the stories of God to others.'[5]

After all the study, I was eager to explore some practical applications and test out these theories for myself. An invitation to offer a programme of five children's sessions to run concurrently with adult meetings seemed like the perfect opportunity. The occasion was a summer conference for an organization called InterChurch Families. My series of sessions was targeted for children between the ages of three and five years old. Within this context I was able, to a certain extent, to implement Berryman's model.

Preparation

We had been asked to work with the same scripture passages that were being considered by the adults. Each of the sessions included a welcome, a telling of the Bible story, a period for individual work, a time for sharing and refreshment, and departure. Because the sessions varied in length, additional activities were sometimes included. Seven children were registered for these sessions. There were two other adults to work with me. We were able to discuss in advance how we would work together.

The subject for session two was the feeding of the five thousand. Since I did not have a Berryman 'script' for this particular story, it was necessary to prepare the material in advance. I referred to each of the biblical references and planned a retelling, based on my study and prayerful reflection (Matthew 14:13–21; Mark 6:30–44; Luke 9:10–17; John 6:1–13).

I also made and collected a set of simple figures and materials to use as the focus of the telling. My set included:
- a green felt underlay 50cm x 40cm
- a strip of blue cotton 50cm x 15cm
- figures drawn and coloured to represent Jesus, two disciples, and several groups of people sitting together
- small clay models of five loaves and two fish

I covered a large shoebox with gold paper in which to store the models and fabric.

A narrative retelling of a session

We had settled ourselves in a circle, on the floor, in the story space in our meeting-room. We had greeted each other and shared the relevant news of the moment. There were seven children ranging from three to five years old and three adults. As storyteller, I had already invited the group to be aware that God was with us in the space, and waited until it seemed right to continue. Now I carefully placed the gold-coloured box in front of me, and continued.

What do you see here? Yes, it is a box… a special box. It is gold. What does it look like to you? Yes, it does look like a present. There are objects inside which we will use today to help us tell stories about Jesus. Stories about Jesus are very special; they are like presents to us.

Gently I removed the lid from the box and placed it to one side.

I wonder what's inside…

I removed the green underlay, unfolded it, and with both hands smoothed it open on the floor in front of me.

What do you think this looks like?

I waited for the group to respond, accepting the responses which came—a cloth, some grass, a towel.

In our story today it will be the grass.

Next I unrolled the piece of blue fabric across the edge of the 'grass'.

What might this be?

The responses came back—the sky, some water, a lake.

In our story today it will be a lake. The water looks clear and peaceful. Here is a figure that might be Jesus.

I drew the figure of Jesus from the box and placed it on the 'grass' near the 'lake'.

Jesus had had some bad news. He went away to a quiet place to think about things.

Drawing two more figures from the box and placing them near Jesus, I continued.

His close friends went with him. They had all been working very hard and needed some time to rest.

I took plenty of time in the telling, placing the figures with care, and waiting until it seemed right to continue. Throughout the telling, I kept my attention on the developing story in the middle of the circle. The group was very focused. We had begun our previous session in the circle like this, aware of God with us, in our midst. This was the first time we had used a story from the box.

Jesus and his friends didn't have much time to be alone together. People had heard about the healing Jesus was doing. They were learning many things from the stories he told. Some people followed Jesus and his friends to the place by the lake.

I brought out figures from the box and placed them on the grass, around Jesus.

More people came…

More figures came out of the box.

…and even more. By evening there were very many people listening to what Jesus was teaching and telling. (Pause.) Jesus' friends became worried.

I moved the figures of the friends near to Jesus.

'It is getting late,' they said. 'And many have been here all day. Send the people home, so they can buy food and have something to eat.'

But Jesus said, 'Give them something to eat yourselves.' The friends were very surprised. 'Are we to go and buy bread for all those people? Do you know how much that would cost? We don't have that much!'

Then Jesus asked them a question. 'Well, what do you have? Go and see.' (Pause.) When the friends returned, they brought to Jesus five loaves…

Five small 'loaves' were brought from the box.

...and two fish.

Two small fish were laid beside the loaves.

Jesus asked his friends to invite all the people to sit down in small groups on the grass. When they were all comfortable, Jesus took the loaves and fish, and raised them up. Looking up to heaven, Jesus blessed the loaves and fish and broke them into pieces. Then he gave them to his friends to share with all the people. Over five thousand people were fed that day.

When everyone had eaten, the friends collected all the broken pieces. They filled twelve large baskets with what was left.

When I reached the end of the story, I sat back for a moment and looked again at the characters in front of me. Then I asked some questions that I also was thinking about.

❖ I wonder what it was like to be there?
❖ I wonder how the friends of Jesus felt?

Some responses were offered. There was also some 'thinking' silence. I asked my last question.

❖ I wonder what people told their friends when they went home?

As we were thinking, I replaced the objects in the box, carefully, and in reverse order. The loaves and fish, the people on the grass, the friends of Jesus, and Jesus himself were all replaced. Next I rolled up the blue cloth and placed it in the box. I folded the green cloth and put it away. Lastly I replaced the lid on the box.

I sat back quietly, took a breath, and then looked up to make eye contact with the members of the group. We talked a bit. I asked them how they felt... what they liked about the story. We wondered together about what it would have been like if our little group had been one of the groups waiting for bread and fish from the friends of Jesus. The children had some ideas about what they might have been doing.

Then one of the children asked if she could use the box and tell the story herself. I was very surprised. I had planned a selection of 'work' from which the children might choose in order to follow on from the story, but this was an unexpected request. With some trepidation, and no little curiosity, I agreed. As the child came and settled herself near me, I invited the group again to make themselves comfortable and to remember that God was with us as we shared the story once more.

Four-year-old Anna placed the box in front of herself, paused a moment and then began. 'What does this look like?' She was using the same language and pattern with which I had begun. 'I wonder what's inside?' Carefully she opened the box and placed the lid to one side.

She removed the green cloth, unfolded it and smoothed it on the ground, using both hands. 'What is this?' she asked. 'Today it is grass.' Next the blue cloth was unrolled. 'What does this look like?' and when we offered our suggestions, she continued, 'Today it is a lake.' Next she brought Jesus from the box and went on with the dialogue. 'Jesus had had some bad news...' Anna continued to retell the story, using very similar language and carefully placing the objects. It was breathtaking for me to watch; the whole group was absorbed in the process. Each time Anna removed a character from the box, she looked at it carefully before placing it on the cloth with real tenderness.

When Jesus asked the friends to 'see what you have', Anna added another personal touch by individually moving the characters back and forth from the groups of people to Jesus.

Once more the loaves and fish were drawn out of the box. When necessary I offered one or two of the phrases I had used before. 'Jesus took the bread and raised it to heaven.' Anna had no hesitation about saying what came next. 'Then he blessed the bread and broke it.' We were all very deeply fed.

Anna followed the story through to the end. She returned all the figures to the box and replaced the lid. When she looked up at the group, she was simply beaming with delight. 'May I do it, too?' asked her five-and-a-half year old brother! And once more the group settled themselves to hear the story.

Before we finished our circle time, we had listened to the story four times altogether—my original telling and three repetitions. Each time the dialogue and use of the characters was carefully and affectionately presented. Each time, quite unself-consciously, the teller added some little touch of personal interpretation. Anna's brother Matthew actually placed the loaves and fish with individual groups on the grass. The fourth teller, four-year-old Sophie, gave Jesus a kiss before returning him to the gold box.

The attention of the group never wavered. By the time the group moved on to take a break and then choose some 'work' to do, we had been sitting together in our circle for nearly 45 minutes. This was a very long time for such a group to remain focused. Later, the two other adult helpers told me they were longing to have a turn telling the story... even after the fourth repetition.

The space for individual work

Following the sharing of the story of Jesus and the loaves and fish, the children were invited to choose their own bit of 'work'. One child took a bag of dolls from the shelf, went into the small tent in the corner, and played happily by himself. Two children chose to work with paints and coloured chalk and large sheets of paper. Four children chose to colour, cut out and assemble their own set of figures similar to the ones used in the story telling. There were paper bags, if not gold boxes, for carrying the finished materials.

We adults chose some work also and joined the children around the work tables. The wondering and conversation continued over the activities, in response to the children's interests. The 'grandmother' on our team was very experienced in working with young children and the observations and questions she shared were most interesting to all of us. I remember this as a particularly comfortable and intimate point in the series of sessions. Each person seemed at ease with their task and content to work on in their individual space.

We closed the session by returning to the circle for a brief sharing of our 'work' and a time for saying goodbye. When the parents arrived at the door, the children rose to join their families.

Tea was being served in the garden to the conference members (as well as to the members of two parallel conferences meeting at the same centre).

A postscript

After the children left, the adult helpers performed the necessary acts of housekeeping and then we drifted down to claim our own refreshment. Imagine my delight and surprise to discover, among the many groups of animated adults in the garden, three small knots of people grouped around three small children with figures and materials carefully being displayed on the ground in front of them.

For most of the rest of the conference, whenever the two hundred people—mostly adults—came together, these same small children were carried on an adult arm or sheltered on a parental lap. On this occasion, however, something overrode their natural reticence. These young children had drawn a group of adults and children around themselves and were retelling the story we had worked with in our session. It was a surprising and awesome moment.

In the words of the psalmist, 'O Lord, our Lord, how majestic is your name in all the earth! You have set your glory above the heavens. From the lips of children and infants you have ordained praise' (sometimes translated as 'strength') (Psalm 8:1–3, NIV).

NOTES

1 Watts, F. & Williams, M., *The Psychology of Religious Knowing*, Geoffrey Chapman, 1988.

2 Winnicott, D.W., *Playing and Reality*, Basic Books, 1971.

3 Hay, D. with Nye, R., *The Spirit of the Child*, HarperCollins, 1998.

4 Berryman, J.W., *Godly Play: an Imaginative Approach to Religious Education*, Augsburg Fortress, 1991.

    See also Berryman, J.W. & Stewart, S.M., *Young Children and Worship*, Westminster/John Knox Press, 1989.

5 Berryman & Stewart, *Young Children and Worship*, pp. 13–15.

∞

CHAPTER TEN

Moving on

Peace, my friends.
May the love of God go with you...
May the Spirit walk beside you...
May you always find your way.

JAIME RICKERT, 'PEACE' FROM CASSETTE *BY YOUR TOUCH: SONGS BY JAIME RICKERT*

One more reflection

We began this book with an invitation to tell our stories and to prepare by spending time at a place of refreshment with others travelling on the way. In these chapters I hope you have indeed found refreshment, reason to celebrate and opportunities to affirm the good practice which has brought you to this point. As we moved through the process of claiming a story, and shaping it, did you become even more aware of the story treasure that you carry with you... even in the small object in your pocket or bag? Did you notice how the invitation to come closer and listen to God's story is all around us... on the streets of our community, in the sky and trees and grass, in the pictures and hangings which we see and make?

As we took time with the scriptures, stepping more deeply into

God's story, did you notice how your own experiences and those of the people with whom you live and work have been woven into stories of the people of God? Perhaps you have claimed a new idea, a new gift. Maybe there is something which you will, at least for the moment, leave behind. Have you found a new companion who will travel along the storytelling road with you? Perhaps your companion is a puppet, or an object, or even a story character through whom you found your own voice in a new way.

We have seen that the fidelity of the storyteller is to the integrity of the story itself. Whether it be a story heard or a story read or an experience lived, it is important to communicate that which has been received—to retell the same 'story'. As we come alongside our children to listen and to speak, this is an important commitment. Our listeners, especially our children, need to be able to rely on *our* words; when we pass on what they share with us, it is important to tell *their* stories accurately.

A gift

Celebrating with children has taught me that receiving a going-home party bag is important. Are you willing to, metaphorically at least, reach out and accept such a bag? If so, please put into your bag, and take along with you, any of the stories and ideas with which we have worked that seem like gifts to you. Use them, shape them, and pass them on in ways that seem just right. I would also like to offer you one more gift... one that is often found in a party bag—a bottle of bubble liquid.

It might be as ordinary as the bottle of bubbles off the shelf at the corner shop. With a wand inside, it is ready for use as an everyday introduction to wonder. Even on a cloudy day, a rainbow of colours can be instantly introduced into a space. Adults and children alike will stop to look, and usually expect to take at least one turn themselves. Such a bottle of bubbles passed around a circle can provide an effective invitation to gentle play. As a 'talking object' it gives members of a group something to do with their hands, and breath, as they introduce themselves.

At the first Holy Fools Event early in 1980, at a time when clowning and storytelling were receiving new energy in the UK, a clown from the north brought down a recipe for making 'bubbles which last'. Bubbles made from this recipe are a bit more durable than the ordinary. They can be blown and shaped and connected with an endless variety of tubes and pipes or tools. One member was running a competition to see how long one of these bubbles would last, stored in a glass jar.

Bubbles from this recipe can also be drawn out to be very long and very large. These great creations, when the mixture is right and the wind is fair, will rise high and float for a long way before popping. Any number of games can be devised to see who can blow the longest, or the largest, or the one that floats the highest. A looped cord, strung between two sticks, can provide a tool for drawing out a bubble which is very long indeed—on a good day it will clear the rooftops. What ideas do you have for playing with these flexible bubbles which last?

The recipe I remember (and use myself) is:

❖ three parts water
❖ two parts concentrated washing-up liquid
❖ one part glycerine

The mixture seems to work best when made in advance and allowed to sit before use. It can be poured into buckets or pans for team-based play. Extra water (and washing-up liquid) is useful to have on hand in case the mixture needs to be thinned… or thickened. Needless to point out, in my hands this is not an exact science. Perhaps you can do better!

I have, however, added one or two touches of my own to bubble-ology. The first is to make bubbles, even without the liquid. Such invisible bubbles, once pointed out to a group, seem to work very well. They pack quite small so you can carry many with you and there always seems to be one around when you need it. Like a story, they can be shaped and shared in an almost endless variety of ways. Each teller, when receiving the bubble, can use it however they want—as a football, like an umbrella, even dividing it into three balls for juggling. The difficulty when juggling with these invisible balls is that they are hard to see once you drop them.

The second idea came at the wedding of the daughter of a friend. The wedding guests were each offered a small bottle of bubbles (rather than a bag of rice) with which to greet the couple. A priest friend of mine suggested that the bubble mixture could be made with holy water, and proceeded to bless the mixture. Since then, I have never been short of Bubbles of Blessing. In your journeying—as storyteller and story listener—may you also receive blessing for everything that may be required of you.

INDEX

BIBLIOGRAPHY

The Banner Box: A National Curriculum Resource published by Herefordshire Council Cultural Services, 1999.

Alden, Barbara, 'Singing' in *The Choral Singers' Companion* by Ronald Corp, Batsford, 1987.

Berryman, J.W., *Godly Play: An Imaginative Approach to Religious Education*, Augsburg Fortress, 1991.

Berryman, J.W. & Stewart, S.M., *Young Children and Worship*, Westminster/John Knox Press, 1989.

Bradt SJ, Kevin M., *Story as a Way of Knowing*, Sheed & Ward, USA, 1997.

Brock, Sebastian, *The Luminous Eye: The Spiritual World Vision of St Ephraim*, a CIIS Publication, Rome, 1985.

Colwell, Eileen, *A Storyteller's Choice: An Anthology for Storytellers*, H.Z. Walck, 1964.

Flanagan, Sabina, *Hildegard of Bingen 1098–1179: A Visionary Life*, Routledge, 1989.

Ginzberg, Louis, *The Legends of the Jews* c. 1913, Jewish Publication Society of America, 1982 edition.

Hay, David with Nye, Rebecca, *The Spirit of the Child*, HarperCollins, 1998.

Lash, Nicholas, 'Performing the Scriptures' in *Theology on the Road to Emmaus*.

Lewin, Ann, 'Tide turn', *Candles and Kingfishers*, Methodist Publishing House

Luke, Helen M., *The Inner Story: Myth and Symbol in the Bible and Literature*, Crossman Publishing, 1982.

Moynahan SJ, Michael E., *Once Upon a Parable*, Paulist Press, 1984.

Sasso, Sandy Eisenberg, *But God Remembered: Stories of Women from Creation to the Promised Land*, Jewish Lights Publishing, 1995.

Sasso, Sandy Eisenberg, *God's Paintbrush*, Jewish Lights Publishing, 1992.

Watts, Frazer & Williams, Michael, *The Psychology of Religious Knowing*, Geoffrey Chapman, 1988.

Williams, Rowan, 'The Literal Sense of Scripture', *Modern Theology 7:2*, January 1991.

Winnicott, D.W., *Playing and Reality*, Basic Books, 1971.

Acknowledgments

We would like to thank all those who have given us permission to include quotations in this book, as indicated in the list below. Every effort has been made to trace and acknowledge copyright holders of all the quotations included. We apologize for any errors or omissions that may remain, and would ask those concerned to contact the publishers, who will ensure that full acknowledgment is made in the future.

Extract from 'Tide Turn' by Ann Lewin, from *Candles and Kingfishers*, published by The Methodist Publishing House, used by permission of Ann Lewin.

Extract from 'Listen!' by Walter de la Mare, from *The Complete Poems of Walter de la Mare*, 1969, used by permission of The Literary Trustees of Walter de la Mare and the Society of Authors as their representative.

Extract from 'Genesis' by Eva Tóth, translated from the Hungarian by Peter Jay, used by permission of Anvil Press Poetry Ltd.